LECTURE READY 3

Strategies for Academic Listening, Note-taking, and Discussion

Authors

Laurie Frazier
University of Minnesota

Shalle Leeming
Academy of Art University, San Francisco

Series Directors
Peg Sarosy
American Language Institute
San Francisco State University

Kathy Sherak
American Language Institute
San Francisco State University

OXFORD
UNIVERSITY PRESS

OXFORD
UNIVERSITY PRESS

198 Madison Avenue
New York, NY 10016 USA

Great Clarendon Street
Oxford OX2 6DP UK

Oxford University Press is a department of the University of Oxford.
It furthers the University's objective of excellence in research, scholarship,
and education by publishing worldwide in

Oxford New York

Auckland Cape Town Dar es Salaam Hong Kong Karachi
Kuala Lumpur Madrid Melbourne Mexico City Nairobi
New Delhi Shanghai Taipei Toronto
With offices in:
Argentina Austria Brazil Chile Czech Republic France Greece
Guatemala Hungary Italy Japan Poland Portugal Singapore
South Korea Switzerland Thailand Turkey Ukraine Vietnam

OXFORD and OXFORD ENGLISH are registered trademarks of
Oxford University Press.

Executive Publisher: Janet Aitchison
Senior Acquisitions Editor: Pietro Alongi
Editor: Dena Daniel
Associate Editor: Scott Allan Wallick
Art Director: Maj-Britt Hagsted
Design Project Manager: Nicoletta Barolini
Cover Design by Delgado and Company
Senior Art Editor: Judi deSouter
Production Manager: Shanta Persaud
Production Controller: Robin Roberson

Student Book
ISBN-13: 978 0 19 430971 4
ISBN-10: 0 19 430971 1

Student Book pack (U.S. sales only)
ISBN-13: 978 0 19 441716 7
ISBN-10: 0 19 441716 6

Printed in Hong Kong
10 9 8 7 6 5 4 3 2 1

ACKNOWLEDGMENTS
Illustrations: Karen Minot: 12, 47, 78, 101

Photography:
Photo Edit Inc.: David Young-Wolff: 2 (car, soda): Michael Newman: 2
(sneaker), 69; Colin Young-Wolff: 2 (skateboard); Jeff Greenberg: 3; Bill
Bachmann, 100; Spender Grant: 56 (computer chess, bomb detecting
robot); Mark Richards: 56 (finger print recognition); Myrleen Ferguson
Cates: 57; Bill Aron: 86; AgeFoto Stock: Raymond Forbes: 2 (iPod);
Roy Morsch, 68 (Asian family); Judi De Souter for OUP: 2 (detergent);
Inmagine: Digital Vision: 100; Creatas: 46; BananaStock: 68 (Caucasian
family); Photodisc: 76; Masterfile: Artiga Photo: 34; Alamy: PHOTOTAKE
Inc: 46; Felix Stensson: 90; Getty Images: AFP: 56; Taxi: 68 (Black family)

Introduction

Lecture Ready: Strategies for Academic Listening, Note-taking, and Discussion trains students for academic success. *Lecture Ready 3* is intended for students at the high-intermediate to advanced level. Students learn how to listen to lectures and take notes effectively, and to communicate with other students in group discussions. Through the use of engaging lectures presented via DVD, students experience the demands and atmosphere of a real college classroom. This preparation enables students to enter a college or university armed with the strategies they need to listen, take notes, and discuss ideas independently and confidently.

Thoroughly Integrated Academic Listening and Speaking

In college and university settings, students not only listen to lectures but also discuss the ideas in the lecture with classmates and the instructor, drawing on the knowledge gained through listening. By integrating academic listening and speaking, this book enriches the training for academic readiness. Students also learn key vocabulary selected from the **Academic Word List**. Vocabulary is first presented in context in a reading passage then practiced throughout the listening and speaking process.

A Focus on Strategies

In order to become proficient listeners and speakers, students need strategies that will help them meet their listening and speaking challenges in and beyond the language classroom. Listening to isolated listening exercises provides only limited instruction; students need to learn a process for each stage of listening. Similarly, rather than simply speaking and being evaluated in response to a question, students need to learn the language and strategies for successfully engaging in classroom discussions—strategies that they can apply throughout their academic career.

In *Lecture Ready,* students learn and practice a variety of listening, note-taking, and discussion strategies before they watch an actual lecture and participate in an extended class discussion about the ideas in the lecture.

Students learn two types of listening strategies:

- strategies for independently preparing for each stage of the listening process—before a lecture, during a lecture, and after a lecture
- strategies for recognizing "lecture language"—the discourse markers, speech features, and lexical bundles that lecturers across disciplines commonly use to guide students in taking in information

Note-taking strategies focus the students' attention on the accurate and concise recording of material delivered during a lecture. They learn that effective note-taking is the cornerstone of effective studying.

Students also learn discussion strategies. These strategies clue students in to university classroom expectations for participation. They also allow students to practice the language necessary for becoming an active member of a classroom discussion.

Academic Readiness

Lecture Ready prepares students for the challenges of academic work by training them in effective study habits. Each chapter focuses on strategies that maximize student achievement at each stage of the lesson.

Students prepare for a lecture by reading something on a relevant topic in one of a variety of formats. The readings introduce vocabulary important for students' understanding of the main lecture material.

Before watching the lecture, students review what they already know on the topic and make predictions. During the lecture, students listen actively and take notes (aided by a structure in the earlier chapters, unaided in the later chapters). After the lecture, students solidify their understanding by using their notes to review and summarize the lecture.

The last step is discussion. Students participate in small group discussions, drawing on the information presented in the lecture.

Visual Listening Materials: Lectures on DVD

During an academic lecture, listeners comprehend by making sense of what they hear *and* what they see. Visual cues such as gestures, movement, and board work are an integral part of the spoken message. Without these visual cues, effective listening is challenging for even the most accomplished student. *Lecture Ready* allows students to fully engage in the lecture experience by watching each chapter's centerpiece lecture on DVD.

The lectures present facts and research findings as well as their implications. The lectures also feature all the characteristics of true academic lectures: natural language, pauses, backtracking, false starts, recapping, filler words, stalling, and other hallmarks of one-way communication. All lectures feature the "lecture language" presented and practiced in each chapter.

Engaging Content

In *Lecture Ready,* students learn about and discuss content from a variety of academic fields—topics that speak to the world they live in. The ten centerpiece lectures contain the type of material found in introductory university courses in five academic content areas: business, media studies, science, psychology, and humanities. Chapter topics are designed to appeal to a wide range of student backgrounds and are conducive to class discussions that draw on multiple perspectives.

Positive Results

Students are more competent and confident when they learn *how to listen* and *how to discuss ideas* using proven strategies for academic success. With *Lecture Ready,* students learn these strategies explicitly, helping them understand and adopt effective techniques for academic progress. Students also gain a familiarity with the vocabulary, lecture language, and atmosphere of a real classroom. *Lecture Ready: Strategies for Academic Listening, Note-taking, and Discussion* enables students to make the transition from textbook lessons to successful encounters with real life academic lectures and discussions.

Organization of the Book

Lecture Ready 3: Strategies for Academic Listening, Note-taking, and Discussion contains five units with two chapters in each unit. Each unit focuses on one field of academic study. Each chapter is built around a lecture from a typical course within the field. In each chapter, students are presented with and practice listening, note-taking, and discussion strategies.

Chapters consist of the following components:

- **Build Background Knowledge**

  Think about the topic, reading passage, vocabulary work, review

- **Prepare to Listen and Take Notes**

  Listening strategy, lecture language, practice lecture (listening strategy practice), note-taking strategy, note-taking strategy practice

- **Listen and Take Notes**

  Predictions, lecture, comprehension, summarizing

- **Discuss the Issues**

  Discussion strategy, strategy practice, discussion

Acknowledgements

We would like to express our appreciation to everyone who helped and supported us during the writing of this book. First, we would like to thank the editorial team at Oxford, with special thanks to Dena Daniel and Pietro Alongi, for their guidance, feedback, and encouragement. We would also like to thank Kathy Sherak and Peg Sarosy for designing the book and guiding us through the process. It was a pleasure to reconnect and collaborate with the excellent teacher trainers at the American Language Institute at San Francisco State University. Thanks also to Moya Brennan, Barbara Mattingly, and Adrianne Ochoa for reviewing lecture content.

Shalle would like to thank her colleagues in the ARC/ESL departments at the Academy of Art University in San Francisco for their ideas and encouragement, especially Kate Griffeath, Jennifer Russell, Bob McDonald, Natasha Haugnes, Kevin Forman, and Marian Shaffner, who facilitated the flexibility she needed to take on this project. She would like to thank Robin Mills for sharing her expertise and insight into the publishing world. Shalle would also like to thank her father Pete, sister Elaine, and brother Dan, for sharing various holidays and family events with *Lecture Ready 3* topic development and rewrites. Finally, Shalle would like to thank her Berkeley family—Ellen, Michael, Jakob, and Zelie—for their unflagging interest and encouragement, and for not saying "Peterman" to her as much as she deserved.

Laurie would like to thank her students and colleagues at the University of Minnesota Center for Teaching and Learning Services, especially Kathleen O'Donovan, whose thoughtfulness, creativity, and enthusiasm have been both a support and an inspiration. She would also like to thank Andrea, Cyndy, Karen, and Pam for listening and sharing their insights along the way. And a big thanks goes to her family, especially Dewey, Stefan, and her mother Merrilyn, for all their patience and support throughout this project.

Lecture Ready Program

The *Lecture Ready* program consists of three components:

Student book

contains the readings, strategy explanations, and exercises for the *Lecture Ready* program.

Audio program

(CDs or cassettes) contains the audio-only targeted lecture language exercises necessary to each chapter. These exercises are marked with the audio icon.

Video program

(DVD or VHS) contains the centerpiece lectures for each chapter and the lecture language exercise for Chapter 8 (visual cues). These exercises are marked with the video icon.

Contents

Listening Strategies	Note-taking Strategies	Discussion Strategies
Recognize lecture language that introduces the topic and presents a lecture plan	Organize your notes by outlining	Express your ideas during a discussion
Recognize lecture language that signals a new idea or a transition to a new idea in a lecture	Use symbols and abbreviations	Ask for clarification and elaboration during a discussion
Recognize lecture language for generalizations and support	Practice noting key words in a lecture	Give your opinion and ask for the opinions of others during a discussion
Recognize lecture language that signals repetition of information for clarification or emphasis	Use a split-page format to organize your notes	Express interest and ask for elaboration during a discussion
Recognize lecture language that signals causes and effects	Note causes and effects	Agree and disagree during a discussion
Recognize lecture language that helps you predict causes and effects	Use arrows to show the relationship between causes and effects	Learn to compromise and reach a consensus during a discussion
Recognize lecture language that signals comparisons and contrasts	Note comparisons and contrasts	Expand on your own ideas during a discussion
Recognize non-verbal signals that indicate when information is important	Represent information in list form	Keep the discussion on topic
Recognize lecture language that signals a definition	Review and practice all note-taking strategies	Indicate to others when you are preparing to speak or pausing to collect your thoughts
Recognize lecture language that signals citations—paraphrases and quotations	Review and practice all note-taking strategies	Support your ideas by paraphrasing and quoting others

Contents

To the Student

If you are planning to enter college or university for the first time, you face two equally big challenges: how to understand the amount of complex content in academic lectures, and how to communicate effectively with classmates and professors.

Lecture Ready 3: Strategies for Academic Listening, Note-taking, and Discussion will help you face these challenges by giving you the strategies you need for success in your academic career. You will learn to do all the things that successful students do—listen actively to lectures, take effective notes, and participate confidently in discussions about the lecture with classmates. While learning these strategies, you will also learn and use common academic vocabulary as well as useful idioms.

Lecture Ready presents lively and interesting lectures on DVD. These lectures are on a variety of topics from many different fields of study. The lectures were created to be just like the lectures that students encounter in a college or university.

What You Will Learn

The **listening strategies** in *Lecture Ready* prepare you for each stage of the listening process. You will learn how to use the knowledge that you already have to prepare to take in new information. You will become familiar with lecture language, which will help you follow the ideas during a lecture. You will learn how to bring together all the information from a lecture so that you can better understand, remember, and use what you have learned. Listening strategies help you get the most out of a lecture.

The **note-taking strategies** focus on the way information can be represented on paper. You will learn about and practice useful methods for taking effective notes during a lecture class. You can practice your new note-taking skills during the lecture, too.

The **discussion strategies** are meant to help you feel comfortable discussing information from the lecture with classmates. Many students feel uncertain about speaking in class because they are not sure what to say, when to say it, or how to say it. With *Lecture Ready,* you can learn what professors expect from you and what you should deliver in return. You will learn specific strategies to make you a more confident speaker no matter what subject you are discussing.

Have fun, and enjoy the academic experiences, challenges, and strategies that *Lecture Ready* has to offer.

BUSINESS

business \\'bɪznəs\\ **The study of making, buying, selling, or supplying goods or services for money**

Chapter 1 | New Trends in Marketing Research

CHAPTER GOALS

- Learn about marketing research: different types and current trends
- Learn a Listening Strategy: Recognize lecture language that introduces the topic and lecture plan
- Learn a Note-taking Strategy: Organize your notes by outlining
- Learn a Discussion Strategy: Express your ideas during a discussion

Build Background Knowledge

Think about the topic

1. Look at these products. Then answer the questions below in pairs.

1. Look at the list of factors to consider when purchasing a product. Which factors are most important when purchasing the items in the picture?

   a. cost   **d.** how it looks, tastes, or smells

   b. health or safety   **e.** the brand (company name)

   c. how well it works   **f.** how it makes you feel

2. Imagine this situation. You are president of a chocolate company. Sales of your most popular chocolate bar have decreased sharply this year. You want to find out what people think about your company and this product. What are some ways you can do this?

2. Read this chapter from a marketing textbook on focus groups and how they are used in marketing research.

Talking to Your Target Market: Focus Groups

For years, marketing experts have used various methods to try to understand why consumers chose to buy certain products. How do shoppers **differentiate** one product from another? What **motivates** a consumer to choose one **brand** over another? Marketing researchers want to understand the decision making processes of consumers. That information can help companies decide how to advertise a product or service; it can also help them design new products or redesign existing products so that they will sell better.

In this chapter we will look at the *focus group*, a type of group interview. It has become one of the main marketing research tools to find out how people in the **target** market feel about themselves and the particular brand, product, or service being researched.

For a focus group, researchers usually find six to twelve volunteers from their target market and

bring them together for one or two hours to answer questions and talk about a product, service, or brand. A skilled discussion leader encourages free discussion but focuses the conversation on the product being researched. To do this, discussion leaders ask a lot of open-ended questions, not simple yes/no or limited choice questions. Open-ended questions allow the group's participants

to answer in their own words and in ways the discussion leader may not expect.

Focus groups usually start with general questions about product type. For example, a focus group for the high school market could be asked, "Which brands of athletic shoes are the most popular with people at your school? Why?" Later they may be asked more specific questions about a particular brand. Discussion leaders may ask for opinions directly with questions like, "Why do you buy Nike shoes?" Or they may try to get at attitudes and beliefs more indirectly with a question like, "What do you think about people who wear Nike shoes?" The focus group's answers to these questions tell researchers a lot about a brand's **image**—the way people think about a brand and the people who use the brand. If a lot of kids in a school wear one brand of athletic shoe, this **suggests** that the brand's image is youthful and popular.

Focus groups allow researchers to talk directly with their target market to find out about their beliefs, attitudes, and feelings; however, there are some difficulties in trying to find out what motivates buying behavior with this method. Participants may not always tell the truth. They may avoid disagreeing with others in the group to appear more friendly and likable. They may also lie to avoid embarrassment.

Another reason the results may be unreliable is that people are not always aware of what motivates their buying behavior. Some factors are completely **unconscious**. In fact, a growing body of psychological research suggests that most people will give **rational** reasons for their purchases when asked, but unconscious emotional needs also **influence** many of their buying decisions.

3. Answer the questions about the reading on page 3. Then discuss your answers with a partner.

1. Why do marketing experts want to learn about how people make buying decisions?

2. What is an "open-ended" question? Why do focus group discussion leaders ask this type of question?

3. Why are the opinions given in a focus group sometimes not helpful to marketers?

4. Match the words with their definitions. Look back at the reading on page 3 to check your answers.

____ 1. differentiate   **a.** based on reasonable, logical thinking

____ 2. motivate   **b.** to have an effect on

____ 3. brand   **c.** a picture; an opinion or concept of something

____ 4. target   **d.** to say or show something in an indirect way

____ 5. image   **e.** directed toward a particular group or person

____ 6. suggest   **f.** to understand the difference between similar things

____ 7. unconscious   **g.** to cause someone to want to do something

____ 8. rational   **h.** the name of a company's product

____ 9. influence   **i.** not aware of oneself; not knowing

5. Discuss these questions in a small group. Share your answers with the class.

1. What do you think a business should be more concerned with: meeting consumers' needs or making a profit? Why do you think so?

2. Choose a popular brand, for example, a brand of clothing, car, or food product. Discuss the target market, the kind of image the brand has, and how the company creates that image.

Review What You Know
To help you get ready to take in new information during the lecture, first think about what you already know about the topic.

6. With a partner, write down three things in your notebook that you have learned so far about marketing research.

Prepare to Listen and Take Notes

1. To help you understand the listening strategy, discuss the situation below and answer the questions.

If you arrive late to class and miss the beginning of the lecture, what information might you miss? Why is this information important?

Listening Strategy

Recognize Lecture Language for Topic and Lecture Plan

At the beginning of a lecture, a professor usually tells you the topic, or what the lecture is going to be about. A professor also usually gives students the lecture plan—a general overview of the material and how he or she plans to present it, like a map of the lecture.

Listen for the words and expressions that professors use to indicate the topic. Also, listen for the words and expressions that professors use to indicate the lecture plan.

Topic lecture language

2. Read the expressions that signal the topic of a lecture. Can you add others to the list?

Today we're going to talk about . . .
What I want to discuss today is . . .
Today's topic is . . .
We'll be looking at . . .
I'll give you an overview of . . .
Last time we discussed . . . , and this week we're going to . . .
In today's class we'll focus on . . .

_____

_____

Lecture plan language

3. Read the expressions that signal the plan of a lecture. Can you add others to the list?

There are a few things we'll be covering today. . . .
We'll start out with . . . , and then look at . . .
I'll be covering two areas in today's lecture. . . .
First, we'll look at . . . , then . . . , and finally we'll move on to . . .

_____

_____

4. Read this lecture introduction. Circle the topic. Then underline and label the lecture language that signals the topic and the lecture language that signals the lecture plan.

....

Hi, everyone. Good morning. Last week, if you remember, we discussed advertising research—the different types, such as motivation research and studies of ad effectiveness, and the rest. You should have it in your notes. Well, this week we're going to talk about product research. There are a few different types, and we won't go into them all, but I'll be covering two areas that are the most popular—new product research, to see if people are interested in a new product that's being planned, and competitive product studies, products that compete with the product your company sells. The second one will be really useful for your final class project.

....

Listen for the topic
and lecture plan

5. Listen to the introductions of three different lectures. First, listen to each introduction and write down the topic lecture language and the topic. Then listen to each introduction again and write down the lecture language that *signals* a plan, and also the plan.

1. Topic lecture language: _____

Topic: _____

Plan lecture language: _____

Plan: _____

_____

2. Topic lecture language: _____

Topic: _____

Plan lecture language: _____

Plan: _____

_____

3. Topic lecture language: _____

Topic: _____

Plan lecture language: _____

Plan: _____

_____

Organize Your Notes by Outlining
Outlining is a way to visually represent the relationships between ideas. Space and indentation show which ideas are main points and which are supporting points. Outlining can help you easily differentiate main points from supporting points so that you can study more effectively.

Outline

6. Look at one student's notes from a lecture on marketing research. With a partner, try to summarize the lecture from these notes. What kinds of marketing research did the professor discuss? What support did the professor give?

> Kinds of market research
>
> Geographic
> > country
> > region
> > > e.g. the midwest
> > urban area
> > > city/suburb
>
> Demographic
> > age
> > sex
> > income
> > education
> > > highest level achieved

7. Read this lecture transcript and take notes in outline form in your notebook.

. . . .

Marketing is a process that involves many strategies and activities. Today, I'm only going to talk about two parts—product and pricing.

The first thing a business needs to decide is exactly what product, service, or idea its customers want to purchase. To do this, businesses need to determine their target market, or in other words, who will buy their product. Once a business understands the target market, it can develop its product to fit what the target market will buy. Second, after a business has developed a product, it must decide how to price it. If a product is too expensive, consumers won't purchase it. If it is too cheap, the business won't make a profit, and it won't make enough money.

. . . .

Listen and Take Notes

Listening Strategy

Predict
To help you get ready for new information and to listen more actively, make a prediction about what the professor will discuss based on what you already know about the topic.

Make predictions

1. **Before the lecture, think about everything you have learned and discussed on the topic of marketing research. What do you expect to learn more about in the lecture? Write three predictions below. Compare your predictions with a partner.**

   1. _____

   2. _____

   3. _____

Follow the lecture

2. **Now follow the lecture and take notes. Be sure to listen for the lecture language that signals the topic and lecture plan.**

Topic: _____

Why it developed: _____

_____

_____

How it works: _____

_____

Examples: _____

_____

Future: _____

_____

_____

_____

3. How well were you able to recognize the lecture language? Check the statement that best describes you. Explain your answer.

_____ I was able to recognize when the lecturer said the topic and plan of the lecture.

_____ I didn't recognize when the lecturer said the topic and plan of the lecture.

4. Use your notes to answer these questions.

1. How is neuromarketing research different from other marketing research?

_____

_____

2. Why do researchers care about which area of the brain is used when looking at an advertisement or looking at a product?

_____

_____

3. In the study about cola taste tests, what were the results of the blind taste test? How did the results change when the brand names were given?

_____

_____

_____

4. Why are some people concerned about the use of neuromarketing research?

_____

_____

_____

Note-taking Strategy

Assess Your Notes
During a lecture, you can sometimes miss an important idea or piece of information. Compare notes with classmates in a study group after the lecture to check that your notes are complete.

5. Were you able to answer the questions in Exercise 4 using the information in your notes? Compare your notes with a few other students. Discuss the differences and help each other fill in any missing information—words, definitions, ideas. Complete your notes.

Discuss the Issues

Discussion Strategy

Express Your Ideas

Many professors in the U.S. will ask students questions during their lectures or in class discussions. Also, students are often expected to express their ideas and opinions with a partner or in small groups.

Active participation in class shows that you are interested in and actively thinking about the course content. It can also help you learn and remember the new information presented in class.

Express your ideas

1. Read the expressions for expressing your ideas. Can you add others to the list?

I think/believe/feel . . .	Here are my two cents . . .
In my opinion, . . .	What I'd like to say is . . .
Here's what I think . . .	Personally, I think/feel . . .
I'd like to say/add/mention . . .	

_____

_____

_____

Practice expressing your ideas

2. In groups of four, read the questions and discuss them. Keep the conversation going until every student has had the chance to practice expressing his or her ideas. Use your own ideas or the ones given below.

1. Talk about some specific television ads that you like. Explain why you like them.

> **Possible Ideas**
> The ads for this product always use good music.
> They are for products that I am interested in.
> My favorite celebrity is in the ads.

2. Talk about a new product you have recently bought. Why did you buy that particular product and that particular brand?

> **Possible Ideas**
> good price   nice packaging
> celebrity advertising   all my friends have it
> better quality than others

Discuss the ideas in the lecture

3. Discuss these ideas from the lecture with your classmates. Remember to use the phrases for expressing your ideas.

1. Describe two print or television ads for similar products made by different companies. For example, compare ads for two different clothing stores, two different car insurance companies, or two different brands of shampoo. Based on the ads, what is the target audience for each product? Do you think they have the same target audience? Why or why not? How do the ads appeal to their target audience(s)?

2. As science helps us better understand how people make decisions, this information will most likely be used to sell products. What are the possible benefits of neuromarketing research for consumers? What are the possible negative consequences?

3. Imagine this situation. Your university has received funding from a political organization to conduct a "neuromarketing style" research study among students. Their goal is to see whether the techniques used for product marketing could also be useful in designing political campaigns. This has created a problem in the university community. Many people are opposed to the study because they feel this type of research is dangerous. They think the information gained from the study could be used to control people without them knowing it. Others feel this study is a good opportunity for your university to earn money and for researchers to better understand how the human brain works. What do you think? Why?

4. Look back at your notes. What was another idea in the lecture that you found important and interesting? Tell the class why you think it is important or interesting and ask for their opinions.

Chapter 2 | Business Ethics

- Learn about business ethics
- Learn a Listening Strategy: Recognize lecture language that signals a new idea or a transition to a new idea in a lecture
- Learn a Note-taking Strategy: Use symbols and abbreviations
- Learn a Discussion Strategy: Ask for clarification and elaboration

Build Background Knowledge

Think about the topic

1. Look at the picture. Then discuss the questions below in pairs.

1. Do you know about any cases of corporate crime? What are they? What happened?

2. How would you define "business ethics"?

The Enron Scandal

Enron Corporation was founded in 1985 and quickly grew to become the world's largest energy trader. By 2000, it was the seventh largest U.S. company, employing 21,000 people in over 40 countries and booking sales of more than $100 billion. Then, in December 2001, Enron went **bankrupt**, leaving its employees and **shareholders**, as well as politicians and the general public, wondering what had happened.

It turns out that Enron failed, many say, because of "get-rich-quick" thinking on the part of the company's **executives**. Reportedly, Enron executives made bad investments and borrowed millions of dollars to cover their losses. Then, it seems the accountants hid these losses and exaggerated the company's profits. When asked questions about Enron's finances, its executives and accountants didn't explain what was going on. Despite their silence, they continued to collect large salaries. In 2000, some top executives began to sell their own shares of Enron stock, their own investments in the company, though the company still seemed to be strong. To many people this was a sign that things were not going well and they began to lose confidence in the company. Investors began to sell their stock in Enron and lenders demanded payment of the hundreds of millions of dollars that Enron owed. Unable to pay these debts, Enron declared bankruptcy and the company collapsed.

In 2004, several Enron executives were arrested and charged with **fraud** and other corporate crimes related to the sudden failure of the company. Investors lost their money and employees lost not only their jobs, but thousands also lost their retirement savings. For example, Bobby and Jerry Dotson were Enron employees whose retirement savings were based largely on Enron stocks. They lost most of their $1.5 million life savings when Enron folded.

Many people are still wondering how this kind of **corruption** could have happened and who is to blame. Part of the blame goes to Enron's accountants for not revealing the company's financial troubles. In addition, the company's board of directors did not pay enough attention to the way Enron did business. Finally, the company's executives showed a lack of **conscience** by not being truthful about the company's financial situation and by using their knowledge of the truth for their own benefit. The Enron **scandal** remains one of the most prominent cases of **white-collar** crime in recent years. In the end, it left many people questioning the honesty of corporate leaders and calling for new laws to demand greater **accountability** of corporate executives and accountants.

Enron and other corporate scandals in the news have increased the public's awareness of the importance of business ethics and has prompted a demand for greater responsibility in our business leaders. Though a poor substitute for the savings and jobs lost due to corporate corruption, it is a significant step in the right direction.

3. Answer the questions about the article on page 13. Then discuss your answers with a partner.

1. How would you describe Enron Corporation's performance for the first 15 years?

2. What caused Enron to collapse?

3. What was the result of Enron's collapse?

4. Match the words with their definitions. Look back at the article on page 13 to check your answers.

____ **1.** bankrupt

    a. your own feeling about whether your actions are right or wrong

____ **2.** shareholder

    b. a person who owns stock (shares) in a company

____ **3.** executive

    c. not having enough money to pay your debts

____ **4.** fraud

    d. a person who has a high position in a business

____ **5.** corruption

    e. the expectation that you will be responsible for your actions

____ **6.** conscience

    f. dishonest or illegal behavior, usually by people in official positions

____ **7.** scandal

    g. the act of tricking or deceiving someone, usually to get money

____ **8.** accountability

    h. an action, situation, or behavior that shocks people

5. Circle the phrase with a similar meaning to the underlined idiom.

As a result of corporate corruption, four executives went to prison for <u>white-collar</u> crime.

a. serious   **b.** business related   **c.** violent

6. Discuss these questions in a small group. Share your answers with the class.

1. Who do you think is to blame for the collapse of Enron? What could have been done to prevent it?

2. Do you know about any cases of business fraud or corruption? Who was involved? What happened?

7. With a partner, write down three things in your notebook that you have learned so far about corporate corruption.

▷ p. 4

Prepare to Listen and Take Notes

Recognize Lecture Language for Transitions

During a lecture, professors often signal when they are introducing or changing topics or ideas.

Listen for transitions—the words and expressions that professors use to indicate when they are moving to a new idea.

Transition lecture language

1. **Read the expressions that signal a new idea or a transition to a new idea in a lecture. Can you add others to the list?**

Let me start with . . .	Okay, let's move on to . . .
Let's start by . . .	Next, I'd like to discuss . . .
First we're going to look at . . .	Let's look at/take a look at . . .
Now let's talk about . . .	Now I want to discuss . . .
Now that we've talked about _____, let's go on to . . .	

Another way that a professor can signal a transition is to ask a rhetorical question. Rhetorical questions are given for the purpose of preparing the listener for the answer. They are not questions that the professor wants students to answer.

How can we explain this? Well, . . .

What does this all mean? Let's look at . . .

Recognize lecture language

2. **Read the excerpt from a lecture about corporate responsibility. Underline the lecture language that signals a transition.**

One effect of the Enron scandal and other cases of corporate crime in the U.S. was the passing of the Sarbanes-Oxley Act. Let's start by looking at the aim of this law. Basically, the goal of Sarbanes-Oxley is to improve the accountability of corporate executives to shareholders and to improve confidence in American companies. Now, let's take a look at some of its requirements. One requirement is that companies establish independent audit committees—independent accountants who are required to report honestly about company finances. If you remember, accounting was a big problem in the Enron case. It also prohibits companies from making loans to their executives. On top of that, it protects whistleblowers—employees who report fraud within the company. Okay, so now that we know what Sarbanes-Oxley entails, I'd like to talk about the effect it's had on businesses. Many people agree that new regulations were necessary, but a lot of businesses have complained that Sarbanes-Oxley is just too expensive to implement.

3. Listen to the beginning of a lecture about the ethical behavior of men and women executives. Then write T for true or F for false next to each statement.

_____ **1.** Corporations with both men and women on the board of directors set the same ethical standards as corporations led by men only.

_____ **2.** Women commit more crimes that involve stealing from their employers.

_____ **3.** Women tend to steal larger amounts of money over longer periods of time.

4. Listen to the lecture again. As you listen, write down the lecture language that signals a transition or a new idea. Then listen once more and write down the idea that follows the transition.

1. New idea lecture language: _____

_____

New idea: _____

2. Transition lecture language: _____

_____

New idea: _____

3. Transition lecture language: _____

_____

New idea: _____

4. Transition lecture language: _____

_____

New idea: _____

5. Transition lecture language: _____

_____

New idea: _____

Use Symbols and Abbreviations
Because professors often speak quickly, using symbols and abbreviations will help you keep up with the lecture. Use symbols and abbreviations in place of full words and phrases in order to write down ideas more quickly.

Use symbols and abbreviations

5. Look at these commonly used symbols and abbreviations. Can you think of any others?

=	equals, is the same	etc.	and so on
%	percent	e.g.	for example
+	and	i.e.	that is
/	or	imp	important
⇓	to go down, decrease, lower	w/	with
⇑	to go up, increase, higher	w/out	without
<	is less than	sb	somebody, someone
>	is more than	sth	something
#	number	b/t	between

6. Think about the words that you might use to take notes in a lecture on business ethics. How could you abbreviate those words?

company – co,

7. Read these sentences from a lecture on business ethics. Take notes in your notebook using symbols and abbreviations to represent words and ideas. Compare your notes with a partner.

1. A whistleblower is someone who reports that his or her own company or business is doing something wrong or illegal.

whistleblower = sb who reports own co/biz for doing sth illegal

2. For example, Jeffrey Wigard and Cynthia Cooper are two executives who exposed corporate crimes.

3. Between 1993 and 2002, the number of workplace theft cases involving women increased by 80.5 percent.

4. An auditor is someone who officially examines the tax records of a business or company—in other words, someone who is required to give an honest and independent report.

Listen and Take Notes

Make predictions

▷ p. 8

1. **Before the lecture, think about everything you have learned and discussed on the topic of corporate ethics. What do you expect to learn more about in the lecture? Write three predictions below. Compare your predictions with a partner.**

    1. _____

    2. _____

    3. _____

Follow the lecture

▷ symbols, p. 17

2. **Now follow the lecture and take notes using symbols and abbreviations to represent words and ideas. Remember to listen for the lecture language that signals a transition.**

Topic: _____

Goals of business ethics: _____

_____

_____

Why people are concerned with business ethics: _____

_____

_____

Impact of corruption: _____

_____

How ethical work environments help businesses succeed: _____

_____

_____

Things a company can do to promote ethics: _____

_____

_____

_____

3. How well were you able to recognize the lecture language? Check the statement that best describes you. Explain your answer.

I was able to recognize when the lecturer moved to a new idea _____.

a. all of the time   **b.** most of the time   **c.** sometimes   **d.** not often

4. Use your notes to answer these questions.

1. What is the goal of business ethics?

_____

_____

2. What are two examples of the impact of corruption on companies and the economy?

_____

_____

3. How can promoting business ethics help a company to succeed?

_____

_____

4. Name three things that can be done to encourage an ethical work environment.

_____

_____

5. Were you able to answer the questions in Exercise 4 using the information in your notes? Compare your notes with a few other students. Discuss the differences and help each other fill in any missing information. Complete your notes.

Note-taking Strategy

Summarize the Lecture
A good way to help remember the information in a lecture is to put the key ideas into your own words. This will also help you confirm that you understood the lecture and that your notes are complete.

As soon as possible after a lecture, put the key ideas into your own words and speak them out loud to a study partner or to yourself.

6. Work with a partner and take turns. Summarize the lecture out loud. Explain the main points of the lecture to your partner. Talk for 2-3 minutes only.

Did you both understand all the points in the lecture? Did you both catch all the information?

Discuss the Issues

Discussion Strategy

Ask for Clarification and Elaboration
It is challenging to follow a classroom discussion, but students are expected to take responsibility when they don't understand what the professor or a classmate says. Politely ask for clarification when you don't understand something, or ask for elaboration to find out more information that will help you understand the topic.

Ask for clarification
and elaboration

1. Read the expressions for asking for clarification. Can you add others to the list?

Sorry, could you repeat that, please?
Excuse me, could you say that again?
Sorry, I didn't catch that. Could you repeat it, please?
Could you please say that a little more slowly/loudly?
Could you explain that?
What does _____ mean?
What do you mean by _____?
Could you go over _____ again, please?
I don't get what you mean by _____.

_____

_____

2. Read the expressions for asking for elaboration. Can you add others to the list?

Excuse me, what is _____?
How does that work?
Why is that?
Can you give me an example of that, please?
Can you tell me more about _____?
Can you describe that for me?

_____

_____

Practice asking for clarification and elaboration

3. In groups of four, do the activity below and discuss the questions. Keep the conversation going until every student has had a chance to practice asking for clarification and elaboration.

Think of a business you have worked in or would like to work in.
- What kind of business is it?
- What kind of work did/would you do?
- How would you describe the work environment (office, retail store, etc.)? How would you describe your co-workers?
- It what ways could your ethics be tested in this business? Use your imagination and think of some possible examples.

Discuss the ideas in the lecture

4. Discuss these ideas from the lecture with your classmates. Remember to use the phrases for asking for clarification and elaboration.

1. The lecture explains that the goal of business ethics is to consider the responsibilities a company has to its stakeholders (employees, shareholders, clients, community) while also making a profit. Do you agree with this statement? If so, why? If not, what do you think the main goal of a business should be? Explain your answer.

2. The lecture suggests that companies write a "code of ethics" for their employees to follow. Imagine you are the president of a company. What rules would you include in your code of ethics? What would you do to make your employees accountable?

3. Do you think that women are more ethical than men? Why or why not?

4. Look back at your notes. What was another idea in the lecture that you found important and interesting? Tell the class why you think it is important or interesting and ask for their opinions.

Unit Wrap-Up

1. **Work in small groups. Do the activity described. Then write a short report on your experience and what you learned from it.**

Happy Cereal Company is introducing a new product—a cereal for children called Healthy Flakes. Healthy Flakes have lots of added vitamins, but also contain a lot of sugar. A community organization opposes the company's use of neuromarketing to develop the advertising campaign to promote the cereal to children. They have arranged a meeting with company executives to discuss their concerns.

Work in small groups with one or two people taking on each of the following roles:

- **Community leader:** You are concerned about the negative health effects on children in the target market (children aged 5–8).
- **Business executive of the company:** You need to maintain a commitment to all stakeholders. You want to maximize profit for the company and shareholders, but also protect the image of the company in the community.
- **Shareholders in company:** You are concerned mostly with earning profits from your investment in the company.

In groups, take turns playing the different roles. Be sure to show you are listening to the other groups by asking for clarification and elaboration.

2. **Work in small groups or with a partner. Conduct a survey of employees outside of class to find out their ideas on ethics in the workplace. Use the questions below or create some of your own. Talk to at least five people, then compile your results and draw some conclusions. Share your conclusions with the class.**

1. Do you think most company leaders want to do what is best for themselves, or what is best for their employees?
2. Do you think your business leader or president is honest? Do you think your supervisor is honest? Do you think most of your co-workers are honest?
3. Do you think women are more ethical at work than men?

unit 2

MEDIA STUDIES

media studies \\'midiə 'stʌdiz\\ The study of the processes by which information is exchanged

Chapter 3 | Trends in Children's Media Use

CHAPTER GOALS

- Learn about changes in media use in society
- Learn a Listening Strategy: Recognize lecture language for generalizations and support
- Learn a Note-taking Strategy: Practice noting key words in a lecture
- Learn a Discussion Strategy: Give your opinion and ask for the opinions of others

Build Background Knowledge

Think about the topic

1. Read the results of this survey about media use among young people. Then discuss the questions below in pairs.

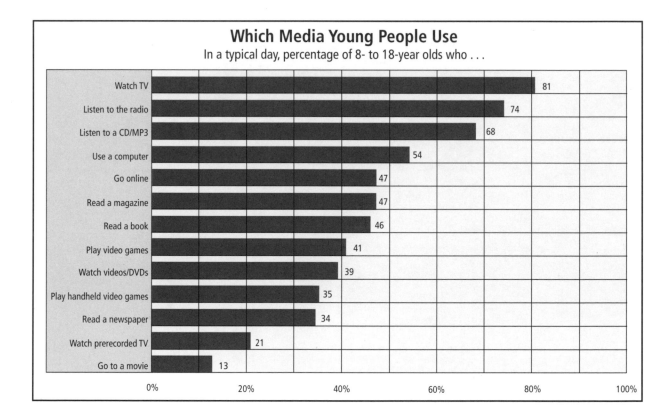

Which Media Young People Use
In a typical day, percentage of 8- to 18-year olds who . . .

Media	Percentage
Watch TV	81
Listen to the radio	74
Listen to a CD/MP3	68
Use a computer	54
Go online	47
Read a magazine	47
Read a book	46
Play video games	41
Watch videos/DVDs	39
Play handheld video games	35
Read a newspaper	34
Watch prerecorded TV	21
Go to a movie	13

1. How does your use of media compare to that of 8- to 18-year-olds in the study?

2. How has your use of media changed in the last five years? Why?

2. Read this report from a consumer survey organization on the characteristics of today's children.

REPORT

The generation of children growing up today has the greatest variety of and access to media than any generation before it. This has made it fundamentally different from past generations in many ways. Here are a few of the key differences:

❐ *Today's children understand and use visual images extremely effectively, but are less skilled at reading and writing texts.*

Because today's children have more **exposure** and access to a greater variety of visual media, they spend less time acquiring knowledge by reading long **texts**. The **constant** presence of images (pictures and videos) have created students who are dependent on pictures and moving images to help them learn. Though their text reading and writing ability may be underdeveloped, they are very good at understanding image-based visual information—an important skill in our increasingly image-based world.

❐ *Today's children can quickly shift their attention from one task to another and do several tasks at one time.*

Children today are not at all afraid of technology. They use it with ease and **confidence**. They are also comfortable with "multitasking"—doing many tasks or using two or more types of media **concurrently**. They can shift their focus from one area to another quickly. Some experts **infer** that these characteristics are having a negative effect on today's children. Others believe these characteristics are natural adaptations to the requirements of their world. A short **attention span** may just show their ability to monitor and control an **intensely** media-rich environment.

❐ *Today's children are connected.*

Communication technology today is oriented toward making social connections **convenient** for users, and today's children are heavy users of this technology. They use text messaging, voice messaging, e-mail, and other electronic means to create strong social connections through constant communication. Consequently, when learning, kids today prefer socially oriented activities where they can work in teams or with classmates and friends.

❐ *Today's children like to learn by experience.*

The current generation of schoolchildren would rather learn by discovering new things for themselves. For example, they are more likely to learn a new software program from experimenting and working with peers than from taking a formal class or reading an instruction book. They approach new technology confidently because they have had so much exposure to different types of new technology in their lifetime.

The quickly changing face of technology in the modern world has resulted in big changes. One change is the decrease in some of the abilities that people once thought were extremely important to a child's educational experience. It has also meant a huge increase in others. Some time is needed to understand the effect these changing abilities will have on society and future generations.

**3. Read these statements about the report on page 25. Then write T for
true or F for false next to each statement. Discuss your answers with a
partner.**

_____ 1. Young people today require more picture-based information to learn
effectively.

_____ 2. Children spend less time interacting with other children because
of increased use of media technology.

_____ 3. The multitasking behavior of children probably only has negative
effects.

**4. Match the words with their definitions. Look back at the report on
page 25 to check your answers.**

_____ 1. exposure	**a.** seeing or being in contact with something
_____ 2. text	**b.** to reach a conclusion from the information you have
_____ 3. constant	**c.** existing or happening at the same time
_____ 4. confidence	**d.** happening or existing all the time
_____ 5. concurrently	**e.** very strongly or seriously
_____ 6. infer	**f.** feeling sure of your own abilities or opinions
_____ 7. intensely	**g.** easy to use
_____ 8. convenient	**h.** The main body of words in a printed or written document, article, book, etc.

5. Circle the best definition of the underlined phrase.

For students with a short <u>attention span</u>, lectures can sometimes feel boring.

a. the amount of time you can
concentrate on something

b. the amount of tasks you have
to do in a period of time

**6. Discuss these questions in a small group. Share your answers with the
class.**

1. Do you think dependence on images and pictures will have a negative
impact on future generations?

2. Do you think multitasking makes you work more or less efficiently? Why?

**7. With a partner, write down three things in your notebook that you
have learned so far about children's media use.**

Prepare to Listen and Take Notes

1. To help you understand the listening strategy, discuss the situation below and answer the question.

You are listening to a long lecture with many ideas. How can you tell the general ideas from the specific examples and explanations that support them?

Listening Strategy

Recognize Lecture Language for Generalizations and Support
Professors often support general ideas in their lectures with research, observations, and stories. Sometimes the generalization comes before the supporting information; sometimes the supporting information leads to a generalization.

Generalizations and support lecture language

2. Read the expressions that signal a generalization or support for the generalization. Can you add others to the list?

This leads us to believe . . .   _____
I hope you can see . . .
We can infer from this that . . .   _____
What can we infer from this? . . .
What can we conclude from this? . . .   _____
This shows/proves/demonstrates that . . .
Let me back this up with a story/some findings. . . .

Recognize lecture language

3. Read these excerpts from a lecture about multitasking. Underline the lecture language that signals a generalization or supporting information.

. . . .

Excerpt 1
There seems to be a connection between emotions and media use. Children who are unhappy use media more. Let me back this up with some findings. One study showed that 18% of young people who scored lowest on the happiness scale,. . . they were the students who reported themselves to be the least happy,. . . they spent more time using media than their happier peers.

Excerpt 2
Only 5% of young people said that their parents had rules about the type of video games they can play. Even though there has been a lot of public controversy in the media about video game content,. . . especially violence in video games,. . . this leads us to believe that this issue is not of great importance to parents.

. . . .

4. Listen to the lecture about multitasking. Then write T for true or F for false next to each statement.

____ **1.** When people change tasks often, they do them more slowly.

____ **2.** Your brain works twice as hard when you are working on two different tasks at the same time.

____ **3.** Multitasking is an important skill in today's office workplace.

5. Listen to the lecture again. As you listen, write down the lecture language that signals a generalization or support. Then listen once more and write down the generalization or the support.

1. Lecture language: _____

Generalization: _____

_____

_____

2. Lecture language: _____

Generalization: _____

_____

_____

3. Lecture language: _____

Generalization: _____

_____

_____

4. Lecture language: _____

Support for generalization: _____

_____

_____

Note Key Words

When listening to a lecture, you don't need to write every word you hear. The best note-takers focus on writing the key words (or important words) for understanding the ideas in the lecture. These are nouns, verbs, adjectives, and adverbs. The key words convey most of the meaning in a sentence.

Note key words

6. Read this excerpt from the transcript of the practice lecture and look at one student's notes. Then, with a partner, use the student's notes to summarize the excerpt without looking at the transcript.

At the University of Michigan they conducted a study with math problems. They found that if students had to switch back and forth between different types of math problems, it took them longer to do them. If they could focus on one type at a time, they could do the problems more quickly. What can we infer from this? Well, that we are less efficient when we multitask that when we focus on one activity at a time.

> U Michigan – study w/ math problems
> Found: if Ss switch b/t diff types probs, took > time
>   if focus 1 type – faster
> Infer?
>   multitask = we < efficient
>   focus 1 activity/time = we > efficient

Focus on key words

7. Read these sentences from the transcript of a lecture about communication and technology. Take notes in your notebook using key words.

1. Because of the increased speed and availability of communication technology, young people today expect a quick answer or response to any communication they send.

2. Another reason they expect a quick response is because they like to multitask and they expect others to be doing the same.

3. If a teenager waits 48 hours for a response, she may feel ignored. A middle-aged person may see this response time as quick.

4. Miscommunication between different age groups can easily happen because of different ideas about communication response time.

Listen and Take Notes

Make predictions

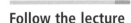 p. 8

1. Before the lecture, think about everything you have learned and discussed on the topic of children's media use today. What do you expect to learn more about in the lecture? Write three predictions below. Compare your predictions with a partner.

1. _____

2. _____

3. _____

Follow the lecture

key words, p. 29

2. Now follow the lecture and take notes, focusing on the most important words. Remember to listen for the lecture language that signals a generalization or support.

**3. How well were you able to recognize the lecture language? Circle the
answer that best describes you. Explain your answer.**

I was able to recognize the lecture language _____.

a. all of the time   **b**. most of the time   **c**. sometimes   **d**. not often

4. Use your notes to answer these questions.

1. What are three ways access to media has changed in the last 50 years?

_____

_____

_____

2. Why did researchers infer that young people today do a lot of multitasking?

_____

_____

_____

3. When a young person has access to media in her bedroom, how does
that change her media use?

_____

_____

_____

4. What are some of the negative effects of increased media use? What are
some of the positive effects?

_____

_____

_____

_____

**5. Were you able to answer the questions in Exercise 4 using the
information in your notes? Were the key words enough to remind you
of the main ideas? Compare your notes with a few other students.
Discuss the differences and help each other fill in any missing
information. Complete your notes.**

**6. Work with a partner and take turns. Review your notes from the
lecture. Then explain the main points of the lecture to your partner.
Talk for 2-3 minutes only.**

Discuss the Issues

Discussion Strategy

Give Your Opinion and Ask for the Opinions of Others
There are often times when you would like to offer your opinion during a discussion. There are also times when it would be interesting or valuable to hear the opinions of others. Use expressions to show that you want to share your thoughts or want others to share theirs.

Giving and asking for opinions

1. **Read the expressions for giving and asking for opinions. Can you add others to the list?**

Giving your opinion

I think/feel . . .
In my opinion, . . .
It seems to me . . .
To me, . . .
In my experience, . . .

_____

_____

_____

Asking for opinions

What do you think about _____?
Alex, how do you feel about _____?
I'd like to hear what Alex has to say.
Does anyone have an opinion on this?
In your experience, [question]
What's your take on this?

_____

_____

_____

**2. In groups of four, read the questions and discuss them. Keep the
conversation going until every student has had a chance to practice
giving and/or asking for an opinion.**

1. Are strong reading skills as important today as they were for you or your
   parents? Why or why not?

2. Consider the following media activities:
   - watching video (television, DVD, satellite/cable)
   - listening to music (radio, CDs, MP3s)
   - Internet use (Web surfing, blogging, e-mail)
   - reading (books, magazines, newspapers)

   Which media activity is the most entertaining for you? Why?
   Which media activity is the most informative/educational? Why?

**3. Discuss these ideas from the lecture with your classmates. Remember
to use the phrases for giving and asking opinions.**

1. How has your use of media changed in the last five years? Has this had
   a mostly positive or mostly negative effect on the following aspects of
   your life:
   - social life
   - school work
   - alone time
   - work
   - other: _____

2. Do you think the increase in the amount of multitasking that children
   do is more harmful or helpful in preparing them for the modern world?
   Explain.

3. When you were growing up, did your parents have rules about using
   different types of media—TV, the Internet, radio, etc.? If so, what were
   the rules? Do you think these rules were appropriate? If not, why not?
   Do you think they should have had rules? What kind of rules would you
   make for your children?

4. Look back at your notes. What was another idea in the lecture that
   you found important and interesting? Tell the class why you think it is
   important or interesting and ask for their opinions.

Chapter 4 | The Changing Music Industry

CHAPTER GOALS

- Learn about how modern technology is changing the music industry
- Learn a Listening Strategy: Recognize lecture language that signals repetition of information for clarification or emphasis
- Learn a Note-taking Strategy: Use a split-page format to organize your notes
- Learn a Discussion Strategy: Express interest and ask for elaboration during a discussion

Build Background Knowledge

Think about the topic

1. Look at the picture of someone using current technology to listen to music. Then discuss the questions below in pairs.

1. Where do you get the music you listen to? How do you listen to it?

2. Decide whether you agree or disagree with the following statement: Downloading music off the Internet without paying for it is no different from buying a used CD or copying a friend's CD. Explain your answer.

2. Read this excerpt from a textbook on business law.

Intellectual Property and the Music Business

The idea that a person can own land, a house, and other possessions is as old as civilization itself. Some of the earliest texts from ancient cultures talk about laws related to ownership. Owning an idea is a more recent invention. Inventors, designers, painters, and musicians all have the legal right to make decisions about the use and sale of their creative work. We call this type of work *intellectual property*. Intellectual property rights related to music and other creative activities, such as books, films, and paintings, are called *copyright*.

There are a lot of questions related to copyright, especially now that so much creative work involves new and **innovative** technologies. What can be owned? How long is it owned? How much effort should be used to **enforce** copyright laws and punish people who break those laws?

With the general public, there is a lot of confusion about what is and is not allowed under copyright law. Recording a television program for later viewing is very common, and most of us have loaned a DVD or a CD to a friend at one time or another. Most people think this is a perfectly legal activity if you are not earning money from it, but some argue the opposite. People are confused, in part, because copyright laws related to new media technologies are unclear. Indeed, today there are many **gray areas** about what is actually legal and what would be considered copyright **infringement**.

In the music industry, one of the more recent issues is related to **distribution**. Sending and receiving music via the Internet, also known as file sharing, is a very common practice today, especially with teenagers and young adults. Most of this activity, however, **violates** U.S. and other international agreements regarding intellectual property.

Many people—most of them not in the music business—believe that downloading and sharing creative works should not be illegal. They feel that strong copyright laws **restrict** the flow of ideas needed to encourage innovation.

Most musicians, and the music companies that produce and **promote** their music, however, argue for stronger copyright laws. Music is a business, and they believe that they should be able to earn money from the products they create. They believe that every person who has a copy of the product—on a computer (MP3 files), on DVD, on CD, or any other format—should pay for it.

To discourage music file sharing, the music industry is always looking for new security devices and technology to restrict file sharing—legal or illegal file sharing. The companies that produce this technology do not support the efforts of the music industry to protect copyright. They feel such devices will restrict the flow of information and limit technological development and innovation. Even some musicians are against restricting people from downloading and file sharing music. They argue that file sharing helps new bands promote their music cheaply and easily. Established musicians, they claim, can continue to make money from live performances and by selling merchandise like t-shirts, posters, and other promotional items.

Despite industry efforts to stop file sharing and illegal downloading, the free flow of information seems to be the way of the future, and impossible to stop. In the years ahead, as the cyber age continues to **democratize** the making and distribution of music, issues surrounding copyright law will surely become increasingly complicated and hotly debated.

3. Answer the questions about the reading on page 35. Then discuss your answers with a partner.

1. Why are copyright laws unclear?
2. How does the music industry in general feel about downloading and file sharing? Why?
3. What are some of the arguments against restricting downloading? Who supports them?

4. Match the word with its definition. Look back at the reading on page 35 to check your answers.

____ 1. innovative   **a.** to limit the freedom, amount, size, etc., of something

____ 2. enforce   **b.** to break the law

____ 3. infringement   **c.** to advertise or make something known

____ 4. distribution   **d.** to allow everyone involved to participate equally

____ 5. violate   **e.** the way of providing something to various people

____ 6. restrict   **f.** using new ways of thinking

____ 7. promote   **g.** the illegal or unfair reduction of someone's rights

____ 8. democratize   **h.** to make sure laws are followed and obeyed

5. Circle the phrase with a similar meaning to the underlined idiom.

As technology changes the music industry, there are many legal <u>gray areas</u> connected to music distribution.

a. old ideas   **b.** unclear situations   **c.** serious problems

6. Discuss these questions in a small group. Share your answers with the class.

1. Some people think that if the cost of buying music (on CDs or downloading) were lower, fewer people would download music without paying for it. Do you agree or disagree? Why?

2. How common is it for people you know (yourself, friends, family) to download music without paying for it? Do you feel it is okay to:
   - borrow a CD from a friend and listen to it?
   - borrow a CD from a friend and copy it?
   - listen to music on the Internet?
   - download music off the Internet without paying for it?

7. With a partner, write down three things in your notebook that you have learned so far about the way technology is changing the music industry.

Prepare to Listen and Take Notes

1. To help you understand the listening strategy, discuss the situation below and answer the question.

While reviewing your notes after a lecture, you notice that there are several places where you wrote down the same idea twice, but in different words. How can you tell when the professor is repeating information?

Listening Strategy

Recognize Lecture Language that Signals Repetition
In a lecture, not all information is new information. Sometimes a professor repeats a point using different words. This repetition is often used to clarify or emphasize a point.

Listen for expressions that signal repetition to help you identify important points and avoid writing the same idea twice.

Repetition lecture language

2. Read the expressions that signal repetition for clarification or emphasis. Can you add others to the list?

In other words, . . .
What I mean is . . .
So, what I'm saying is . . .
That is, . . .

Which is to say, . . .
As I said, . . .
Let me restate that: . . .
Let me say that another way: . . .

_____

_____

_____

_____

Recognize lecture language

3. Read the excerpt from a lecture about copyright law. Underline and label the original phrase, the lecture language that signals the repetition, and the new phrase.

. . . .

There have been many legal battles between media and technology companies in recent years. In 1984, the U.S. Supreme Court decided that Sony was not legally responsible for the illegal uses of the video recorder they created. Which is to say, Sony, or any company, is not to blame when people use its inventions to break the law, . . . especially when there are many ways that the invention can be used legally. They said that it was true that many people use the video recorder to tape and distribute video illegally, but they also use it for activities that do not violate copyright law. So, in other words, people will use equipment for legal and illegal purposes, and the equipment maker has no control over that.

. . . .

4. Listen to the lecture about copyright law. Then write T for true or F for false next to each statement.

_____ **1.** Everyone agrees strong copyright laws are good for society.

_____ **2.** Copyright law was created so innovators would be financially motivated to create new things.

_____ **3.** Today, copyright protection ends when the creator dies.

5. Listen to the lecture again. As you listen, write down the lecture language that signals repetition for clarification or emphasis. Then listen once more and write down the new way the professor makes the point.

1. Lecture language: _____

Repeated point: _____

2. Lecture language: _____

Repeated point: _____

3. Lecture language: _____

Repeated point: _____

4. Lecture language: _____

Repeated point: _____

5. Lecture language: _____

Repeated point: _____

Note-taking Strategy

Use a Split-Page Format
The split page note-taking method is a useful way to arrange your notes so that you can easily review information later and study for exams.
Divide the page into two sections by drawing a line from top to bottom. On the right side, take notes as usual. Leave the left side blank. After the lecture, review your notes and write possible exam questions, reminders, and summaries in the blank space. (Be sure to review your notes within 24 hours of the lecture.) The information you write on the left side will help you when the time comes to study for exams.

6. Read the transcript from a lecture about some of the problems of copyright. Then look at one student's notes below. Write questions, comments, or anything you feel would be valuable later, on the right. Compare your work with a partner.

. . . .

As you know, copyright law is about protecting "intellectual property" . . . it's about ownership of creative products like music, literature, and art. And we know that in the U.S., the original amount of copyright, . . . ownership time, . . . was 17 years. This is the amount of time set down in the Constitution. Now, copyright applies to most creative works for closer to 200 years. New legal gray areas have been created by new technology. These legal battles are being fought between media companies . . . like music companies, film companies . . . that sell creative products like music and films . . . and tech and electronics companies that create and sell things like software and media players . . . like DVD players. The media companies want to protect copyright so they can make money. They need these profits to pay the artists and continue to provide quality content. The tech and electronic companies feel they are being forced to create devices that restrict the easy sharing of information, and concern about copyright profits are restricting technological innovation.

. . . .

Review	Notes from class
What exactly is copyright?	Copyright (CR)
	= owning intellectual property (music, lit., film)
	US: time 17 ⟶ ~200 years
	Laws: legal gray area
	2 sides
	Media co's (film, music, etc.)
	Want strong CR- $ for artists/make quality prod.
	Tech/electronic co's (software, DVD makers, etc.)
	Want < CR concern-focus on $ means < tech innovation

Listen and Take Notes

Make predictions

1. Before the lecture, think about everything you have learned and discussed on the topic of changes in the music industry. What do you expect to learn more about in the lecture? Write three predictions below. Compare your predictions with a partner.

   1. _____

   2. _____

   3. _____

Follow the lecture

split-page
format, p. 39

2. Now follow the lecture and take notes using the split page method. Remember to listen for the lecture language that signals repetition for clarification and emphasis. After listening and taking notes on the right, review your notes and write study questions, comments, or summaries of the information on the left.

3. How well were you able to recognize the lecture language? Circle the answer that best describes you. Explain your answer.

I was able to recognize the lecture language _____.
a. all of the time   **b.** most of the time   **c.** sometimes   **d.** not often

4. Use your notes to answer these questions.

1. Regarding recording, how has the music industry been democratized in recent years?

_____

_____

_____

_____

2. How has promotion changed in recent years?

_____

_____

_____

3. Explain the different perspectives of technology companies and music companies regarding copyright laws.

_____

_____

_____

_____

_____

_____

_____

5. Were you able to answer the questions in Exercise 4 using the information in your notes? Compare your notes with a few other students. Discuss the differences and help each other fill in any missing information. Complete your notes.

6. Work with a partner and take turns. Review your notes from the lecture. Then explain the main points of the lecture to your partner. Talk for 2-3 minutes only.

Discuss the Issues

Discussion Strategy

Express Interest and Ask for Elaboration
The goal of a discussion is to explore a topic deeply by having participants share their ideas, opinions, and experiences related to a topic. You can show that you are listening to their ideas by offering a response (rejoinder) that shows your feelings about the ideas being expressed. Also, an active participant will encourage others to elaborate on their ideas by asking follow-up questions related to their ideas. These can be general questions (who?, what?, when?, etc.) or more detailed questions that reference their original ideas. Follow-up questions help you learn more about other people's ideas and experiences and keep a discussion going.

Express interest and ask for elaboration

1. **Read the expressions for responding and for asking follow-up questions. Can you add others to the list?**

Responses (Rejoinders)

Interested	**Surprised**
I see.	You're kidding!
That's nice.	Really?
Oh, yeah?/Yeah?	No way!
Uh-huh.	Wow!
_____	_____
_____	_____

Follow-up questions
Who . . . ?
What . . . ?
Where . . . ?
When . . . ?
How . . . ?
Why?
What kind of . . . ?
Can you tell me more about . . . ?
You mentioned _____. What/where/etc. . . . ?

_____

_____

_____

Practice asking follow-up questions

2. In groups of four, read the questions below and discuss them. State your ideas briefly so that the other members can ask you to elaborate. Be sure to use rejoinders as you listen to keep the conversation going.

Example

Student A: I bought the new Alicia Keys CD last week.
Student B: I don't know much about her. What kind of music does she sing?
Student A: This CD is really nice soul music.
Student C: Really? Do you like this CD more than her pop music CDs?

1. What was the last song or collection of songs you bought?

2. What was the first song or album you ever bought?

3. Name one of your current favorite musicians or musical groups.

Discuss the ideas in the lecture

3. Discuss these ideas from the lecture with your classmates. Remember to ask follow-up questions and respond to their ideas.

1. Do you mostly buy CDs or download music? Why do you prefer to get music this way?

2. Do you think it's okay to share digital music files via the Internet? Why or why not?

3. If musicians can no longer sell their songs, what other way could they earn money from their music? In your group, come up with a new model for paying musicians for their work.

4. Look back at your notes. What was another idea in the lecture that you found important and interesting? Tell the class why you think it is important or interesting and ask for their opinions.

Unit Wrap-Up

1. **Follow the instruction to conduct a survey about the media use of children and/or young adults compared with the media use of older generations.**

   - As a class, come up with four or five questions about media usage.

   - On your own or with a partner, survey at least five people in each of the following age groups: 15–24, 25–34, 35–50, and over 50.

   - Discuss your results in a small group. Decide on three general conclusions you can infer from the information.

   - Compare your results and conclusions with the other groups.

2. **As a class, brainstorm the positive and negative effects of strict copyright enforcement on music distribution. Then in small groups, role-play a debate between music recording artists who are for strict copyright enforcement and the inventors of new technology who are against it.**

3. **Interview teachers to find out whether they believe increased media use affects student performance.**

   Arrange to talk to at least two different teachers who have been teaching for more than ten years. Ask them about the differences between students today and students ten years ago.

   - What skills and abilities are stronger?

   - What skills and abilities are weaker?

   - What do they think are the causes of the changes?

   - What role, if any, do they believe increased media use has played in these changes?

   Report your findings in a small group. How closely do the answers from various teachers match? Can any conclusions be drawn from these findings? Share your results with the class.

SCIENCE

science \\'saɪəns\\ **A system of knowledge concerned with the physical world and its phenomena**

Chapter 5 | The Placebo Effect

CHAPTER GOALS

- Learn about alternative medicine and the use of placebos in medical research and practice
- Learn a Listening Strategy: Recognize lecture language that signals causes and effects
- Learn a Note-taking Strategy: Note causes and effects
- Learn a Discussion Strategy: Politely agree and disagree during a discussion

Build Background Knowledge

Think about the topic

1. Look at the pictures. Then discuss the questions below in pairs.

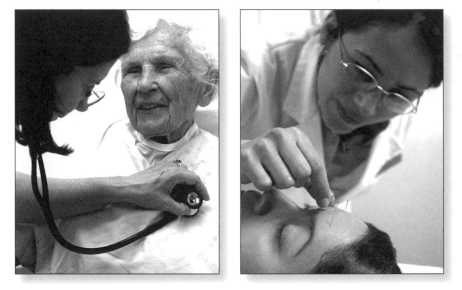

1. What is happening in each of these pictures? How are the activities the same? How are they different?

2. Which qualities in a medical doctor or other health care provider are most important to you? Rank the following qualities in order of importance, with 1 as most important.

_____ honesty
_____ intelligence
_____ compassion
_____ training or schooling
_____ years of experience
_____ knowledge of scientific research
_____ knowledge of a variety of medicines and treatments
_____ other: _____

What Is Homeopathy?

Homeopathy is an approach to medicine that was developed in the 18th century by the German physician, Samuel Hahnemann. He was unhappy with the medical treatments most commonly used at that time. These included blood-letting, in which doctors would drain blood from the patient in order to rid the body of its illness; "blistering" or burning the skin; and feeding patients dangerous chemicals to cause vomiting. Many of these treatments did more harm than good to patients.

The world "homeopathy" actually comes from the Greek words *homoios* (similar) and *pathos* (suffering). This approach involves **prescribing** drugs that copy the symptoms of an illness. For example, if a patient in complaining of headache and nausea, the homeopath will find a drug, often made from plants, herbs, or other natural substances, that is **associated with** causing the same symptoms in healthy people. The theory is that by producing symptoms associated with the illness, the illness itself will eventually be cured. This is in contrast to conventional, or allopathic, medicine, which seeks to produce effects that are different from the symptoms of the disease or illness.

The classic way to make homeopathic remedies is to take one grain of the desired herb or plant and grind it up with ninety-nine grains of milk sugar. The solution is further diluted with more milk sugar until the thirtieth dilution is reached. Similarly, liquid remedies are diluted with water or sometimes alcohol. In the final mixture, it is not possible to **detect** even a single molecule of the starting remedy.

Because homeopathic remedies often contain undetectable amounts of active ingredients, most scientists say that it is impossible to create well-designed studies of their effectiveness.

Since scientists cannot **analyze** or explain how it works, most have rejected homeopathy as **sham** treatment. Still, **clinical trials** of homeopathic remedies have provided some **empirical** evidence that homeopathy can produce positive results in patients. Supporters of homeopathy tend not to be concerned with the **physiological** mechanisms behind this **phenomenon**, they only care that it works for them.

Homeopathy is popular throughout the world. It is most common in Europe and Asia, especially India. In the United States, homeopathy was quite popular in the 19th and early 20th centuries. Since then, most Americans have become **biased** towards allopathic medicine, and most trained doctors do not prescribe or recommend homeopathic remedies. Even so, homeopathy has been again increasing in popularity in recent years. The number of homeopaths in the U.S. increased from fewer than 200 in the 1970s to approximately 3,000 in 199? and is continuing to rise.

3. Answer the questions about the reading on page 47. Then discuss your answers with a partner.

1. What is the main theory behind homeopathy?

2. How are homeopathic remedies made?

3. Why do many scientists and doctors reject homeopathy?

4. Match the words with their definitions. Look back at the reading on page 47 to check your answers.

____ **1.** prescribe		**a.** preferring one side of an argument; not neutral
____ **2.** associated with		**b.** to notice something that is difficult to see, feel, etc.
____ **3.** detect		**c.** a study in which researchers test a treatment on volunteers and carefully monitor the effects
____ **4.** analyze		**d.** something that happens or exists
____ **5.** sham		**e.** relating to how the bodies of living things work
____ **6.** clinical trial		**f.** to recommend a medicine or treatment
____ **7.** empirical		**g.** not valid, not real
____ **8.** physiological		**h.** based on experiments or practical experience rather than ideas or theories
____ **9.** phenomenon		**i.** to be connected with something else
____ **10.** biased		**j.** to look at the different parts of something carefully in order to try to understand it

5. Discuss these questions in a small group. Share your answers with the class.

1. Why do you think people used the common treatments of Hahnemann's time if they were harmful?

2. Have you ever used homeopathy? If so, did it work for you? If not, would you consider using it? In what situations?

3. Do you think homeopathy is a sham treatment? Why or why not?

6. With a partner, write down three things in your notebook that you have learned so far about homeopathy.

Prepare to Listen and Take Notes

1. To help you understand the listening strategy, discuss the situation below and answer the question.

During a lecture, the professor talks about many causes and effects. What language signals would help show the connection between the ideas?

Recognize Lecture Language for Cause and Effect
Professors often explain things in terms of causes and effects. This is to help students understand the relationship between different ideas, events, or phenomena.

Listen for the expressions that professors use to signal causes and effects.

Cause and effect lecture language

2. Read the words and expressions that signal causes and effects. Can you add others to the lists?

Causes	Effects
What's the cause of this? Well, . . .	This leads to . . .
Why is this? Well, . . .	As a result, . . .
This comes from (the fact that) . . .	One effect of this is . . .
This is due to . . .	This produces/results in . . .
The reason(s) for this is . . .	Consequently, . . .
One explanation is . . .	After [cause], then . . .
This is caused by . . .	Because of [cause], (then) . . .
This came as a result of . . .	If [cause], then . . .

_____   _____

_____   _____

Recognize lecture language

3. Read the excerpt from a lecture on homeopathy. Underline and label the lecture language that signals cause and effect with C for cause or E for effect.

· ·

Then, there was a doctor named Samuel Hahnemann who began to develop his own theory, which was based on three principles: the law of "similars," the minimum dose, and the single remedy. The law of similars came as a result of Hahnemann's observations. He noticed that after taking a strong dose of the malaria treatment quinine, he developed symptoms similar to the symptoms of malaria. This led Hahnemann to believe that if a large amount of a substance causes symptoms in a healthy person, then smaller amounts of the same substance can treat those same symptoms in an ill person.

· ·

4. Listen to a lecture on alternative medicine. Then write T for True or F for False next to each statement.

____ **1.** Alternative medicine includes conventional practices such as homeopathy, traditional Chinese medicine, and chiropractic medicine.

____ **2.** There has been a rising interest in alternative medicine in western countries in recent years.

____ **3.** Alternative remedies emphasize the use of chemical drugs.

____ **4.** "Integrative" medicine offers alternative medicine along with conventional medicine.

5. Listen to the lecture again. As you listen, write down the lecture language that signals cause or effect. Then listen once more and write down the actual cause or effect. Circle the correct label.

1. Lecture language: _____

Cause/effect: _____

2. Lecture language: _____

Cause/effect: _____

3. Lecture language: _____

Cause/effect: _____

4. Lecture language: _____

Cause/effect: _____

Cause/effect: _____

Note-taking Strategy

Note Causes and Effects
When listening to a lecture in which causes and effects are presented, list the causes and effects separately under the idea, event, or phenomenon.

Note causes and effects

6. Look at one student's notes from the practice lecture on alternative medicine. Then answer the questions below.

Possible Causes
- people aging; looking for ways to deal w/ long-term health probs.
- recent trend ⟶ natural products, "safer than chemicals"
- people more individualistic, not accept MDs; more educated, want to make own decisions
- immigration – East to West (e.g. China); bring traditional med.

Effects of Rising Int. in Alt. Med
- huge ↑ in # of people practicing alt. medicine; "integrative" medicine
- ↑ testing alt. meds. & holding to rules of evidence (e.g. clin trials)

1. Did this student capture all the causes and effects in his notes?

2. How did he indicate the individual causes and effects? Are they clear enough? How would you do this?

7. Work with a partner. Take turns reading aloud this excerpt of a lecture about chiropractic medicine. While one of you reads, the other takes notes. Then switch roles. When you are finished, compare your notes. Did you catch all of the causes and effects?

Chiropractic is a form of alternative medicine that focuses on the relationship between the body structure, . . . mainly the spine, . . . and overall health. Chiropractors try to prevent and treat health problems by adjusting the spine. Now, many medical doctors and scientists have dismissed chiropractic medicine as ineffective and even dangerous. So why is this? One reason is that chiropractic adjustments can cause serious injuries, especially in the neck and back. Another criticism comes from the fact that some chiropractors extensively use x-ray photography, which can harm patients. Some medical doctors criticize chiropractic treatment because they believe it simply isn't effective, . . . it just doesn't work. Because of these criticisms, the American Medical Association has consistently opposed the use of chiropractic treatment, and it remains a controversial issue in the medical community.

Listen and Take Notes

Make predictions

 p. 8

1. Before the lecture, think about everything you have learned and discussed on the topic of alternative medicine. What do you expect to learn more about in the lecture? Write three predictions below. Compare your predictions with a partner.

1. _____

2. _____

3. _____

Follow the lecture

cause/effect, p. 51

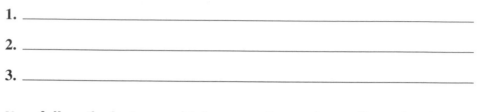

2. Now follow the lecture and take notes. Remember to listen for the lecture language that signals causes and effects.

3. How well were you able to recognize the lecture language? Circle the statement that best describes you. Explain your answer.

I was able to recognize when the professor discussed causes or effects _____.
a. all of the time   **b.** some of the time   **c.** none of the time   **d.** not sure

4. Use your notes to answer these questions.

1. What is the placebo effect? How were placebos used in the past? How are they currently used?

_____

_____

_____

2. What's the difference between a blind test and a double-blind test?

_____

_____

_____

3. What are three possible causes of the placebo effect?

_____

_____

_____

4. Describe the depression study. What did researchers find as a result of this study?

_____

_____

_____

5. Were you able to answer the questions in Exercise 4 using the information in your notes? Compare your notes with a few other students. Discuss the differences and help each other fill in any missing information. Complete your notes.

6. Work with a partner and take turns. Review your notes from the lecture. Then explain the main points of the lecture to your partner. Talk for 2-3 minutes only.

Discuss the Issues

Discussion Strategy

Agreeing and Disagreeing
During a group discussion, you can show your understanding of the topic and the ideas expressed by others by politely agreeing or disagreeing and adding your own ideas. Agreeing with someone is a polite way to acknowledge a good point before you expand on it. A polite way to disagree is to acknowledge a point before you explain another view on the topic. Use expressions to politely agree or disagree with others in a discussion.

Agree and disagree

1. **Read the expressions for agreeing and disagreeing. Can you add others to the list?**

   To agree with others
   Yes, yes, that's true . . .
   That's a good point . . .
   I agree with _____.
   I agree, and . . .
   I totally agree . . .
   I see your point . . .
   She/he is right, . . .
   I think you're right that . . .

   _____

   _____

   _____

   To disagree with others
   I see your point, but . . .
   I see what you mean, but I think . . .
   That's a good point, but it seems to me that . . .
   I'm sorry, but I have to disagree with you on that . . .
   Yes, but I see it a different way . . .
   Okay, but what about . . . ?
   But don't you think . . . ?

   _____

   _____

   _____

Practice agreeing and disagreeing

2. In groups of four, read the question and discuss it. Keep the conversation going until every student has had a chance to practice using the language for agreeing and disagreeing.

What do you think are the three most important considerations when choosing a medical treatment? Use the list below or come up with your own ideas.

_____ it is scientifically proven to work

_____ it has few known side effects

_____ it is affordable

_____ it has helped people you know

_____ you understand how it works

_____ your doctor recommends it

_____ it is the most common treatment for your condition

_____ it has made you feel better before

_____ it is natural (doesn't involve using chemical drugs)

_____ other: _____

Discuss the ideas in the lecture

3. Discuss these ideas from the lecture with your classmates. Remember to use the phrases for agreeing and disagreeing.

1. What do you think causes the placebo effect? Why?

2. Do you think it is ethical for doctors to prescribe placebos to their patients? Why or why not? How would you feel if you found out later that your doctor had given you a placebo?

3. The study mentioned in the lecture demonstrated that some people suffering from depression experienced physiological changes when given a placebo to treat their condition. Why do you think that happened? What do you think is the best treatment for depression?

4. Look back at your notes. What was another idea in the lecture that you found important and interesting? Tell the class why you think it is important or interesting and ask for their opinions.

Chapter 6 | Intelligent Machines

CHAPTER GOALS
- Learn about artificial intelligence
- Learn a Listening Strategy: Recognize lecture language that helps you predict causes and effects
- Learn a Note-taking Strategy: Use arrows to indicate causes and effects
- Learn a Discussion Strategy: Compromise and reach a consensus during a discussion

Build Background Knowledge

Think about the topic

1. Look at the pictures. Then discuss the questions below in pairs.

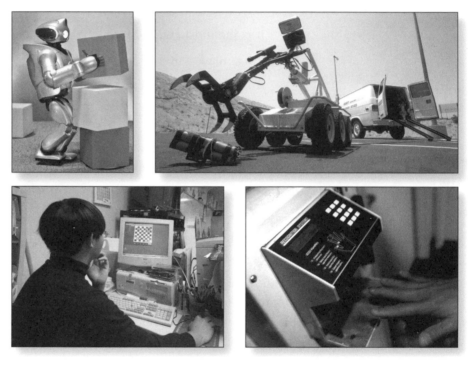

1. Describe the different machines. What do you think each is capable of doing? What do you think makes each one "intelligent"?

2. What do you think are the biggest challenges in developing intelligent machines?

2. Read this article from a science magazine about the development of artificial voices and how human psychology is now driving research.

Artificial Voices

People have attempted to **simulate** human voices in machines for quite some time. In the late 1700s, Hungarian scientist Wolfgang von Kempelen used whistles, resonance chambers, and other objects to create voice sounds for his "Speaking Machine." With the rise of computers, scientists were able to create artificial voices by storing and digitally **processing** real voice sounds. By the 1970s, these computer-generated voices were widely used. Although these early voices were understandable, they had a distinct mechanical or "robotic" sound to them.

Coming up with more natural-sounding voices has been a challenge due to the **complex** nature of language. To produce a natural-sounding voice, scientists need to simulate not only the individual sounds of a language, but also the volume, pitch, rhythm, and tones that help to express meaning. Natural-sounding computer voices are now used to provide information to people in a variety of applications, from automated phone lines to language learning programs. Many systems are also able to listen to users' questions and statements and respond to them.

One good example of this comes from the BMW car company. BMW has programmed cars to both listen and speak to the driver. The car can give directions, provide warnings and information about traffic and safety conditions, and even control certain functions, such as raising or lowering the windows or playing music. When BMW first released cars with a computer-generated voice, many drivers had a negative reaction to it because drivers **perceived** the voice as female. German drivers were uncomfortable with a "female" voice

giving directions. As a result, BMW recalled the cars and gave them "male" voices.

The reaction to the female voice was emotional. It had no **reasoning** behind it. **Common sense** says that the "gender" of the voice in the car shouldn't matter because drivers know that they are listening to a computer, not a person. But even without a **visual** representation of the voice, such as a male or female face, people reacted with the same stereotypes they would apply to a person. Studies have also shown that people react similarly to other aspects of computer voices, such as the "personality" of the voice or its level of "politeness."

Researchers now know that voice **interfaces** are actually social interfaces; that is, people will react to a computer using the same rules and expectations that they would apply to people. As a result, designers of these systems consider not only the sounds of the voices they use, but also their psychological effect on users.

3. Answer the questions about the article on page 57. Then discuss your answers with a partner.

1. Why has it been challenging to create natural-sounding voices in machines?

2. What happened when BMW used a "female" voice to give directions in its cars?

3. What did scientists discover about how people react to computer voices?

4. Match the words to their definitions. Look back at the article on page 57 to check your answers.

____ 1. simulate	**a.** the way a computer program shows information to or receives information from a user
____ 2. process	**b.** the ability to make sensible decisions based on life experience, not schooling or training
____ 3. complex	**c.** connected with seeing
____ 4. perceive	**d.** to use a computer or machine to change or manipulate raw material
____ 5. reasoning	**e.** to think of something in a particular way
____ 6. common sense	**f.** judgment or opinion based on logic or careful thought
____ 7. visual	**g.** made up of many connected parts; complicated
____ 8. interface	**h.** to create the effect or appearance of something else

5. Circle the phrase with a similar meaning to the underlined phrase.

For years, scientists ha ve tried to <u>come up with</u> human-like machines.
a. understand   **b.** create   **c.** advance

6. Discuss these questions in a small group. Share your answers with the class.

1. The reading mentions that German drivers preferred to get directions from a "male" artificial voice. What other types of information do you think people would prefer to receive from a male voice? What types of information would people prefer to get from a female voice?

2. What are some of the benefits of using computer-generated voices? What are some of the drawbacks? Do you think computer voices should be made to sound exactly like human voices? Why or why not?

▷ p. 4

7. With a partner, write down three things in your notebook that you have learned so far about artificial intelligence.

Prepare to Listen and Take Notes

Listening Strategy	**Predict Causes and Effects** Active listeners anticipate what they will hear next so that they can organize the information in their minds and their notes. In Chapter 5, you learned how to recognize lecture language that signals cause and effect. In this chapter, you will practice using that knowledge to predict causes and effects in a lecture. Predict causes and effects to help you think about the relationships between ideas in a lecture while you listen.

Predict cause and effect

1. **Read the first part of each excerpt from a lecture on artificial voices. Underline the lecture language and label it C for cause or E for effect. Then make a prediction about what the professor might discuss next. Discuss your predictions with a partner.**

   Excerpt 1
   Scientists have developed machines that not only speak, but also listen and recognize human speech. This has led to…

   Prediction: _____

   _____

   _____

   Excerpt 2
   But because cars can interact with drivers, scientists must consider…

   Prediction: _____

   _____

   _____

2. **Read the second part of the excerpts above in the Answer Key. Did your predictions match the actual causes or effects? If not, were your predictions logical possibilities? Share your predictions with the class.**

3. Listen to four excerpts from a lecture on computer voices in cars. Follow these steps for each excerpt:

- As you listen, write down the lecture language for cause or effect.
- Pause the recording when you hear the tone.
- With the recording paused, circle what you expect the professor to give next: a cause or an effect. Then write a prediction about the information to come.
- Start the recording again and listen to the end of the excerpt. Write the actual cause or effect and check your prediction.

1. Lecture language: _____

Cause/effect: _____

_____

Actual cause/effect: _____

_____

2. Lecture language: _____

Cause/effect: _____

_____

Actual cause/effect: _____

_____

3. Lecture language: _____

Cause/effect: _____

_____

Actual cause/effect: _____

_____

4. Lecture language: _____

Cause/effect: _____

_____

Actual cause/effect: _____

_____

Use Arrows to Show the Relationship between Causes and Effects
One way to show the relationship between causes and effects in your notes
is to use arrows. For clarity, an arrow should always point *toward the effect*.

Use arrows

4. Read these sentences from the lecture on computer voices in cars. Take notes using arrows to show causes and effects.

1. The designers of the voice for BMW avoided having the car voice use the word "I," as in "I think you should slow down." The reason for this was that they didn't want the car to sound like it was in charge.

    BMW avoided having car voice say "I" (e.g. "I think you should slow down.") ⟵ didn't want car to sound in charge.

2. People also expect the voice in a car to "match" their expectation of the voice's personality. As a result, BMW chose a voice that was determined to sound friendly, but also very competent.

    _____

    _____

    _____

3. One problem with using voices in a car is that, due to the noisy environment of a car, the computer will often have difficulty understanding the driver.

    _____

    _____

    _____

4. The researchers found that drivers were not happy when the voice in the car accepted blame or blamed the driver for misunderstandings. Because of these findings, they chose language that did not include any blame.

    _____

    _____

    _____

Listen and Take Notes

Make predictions

▷ p. 8

1. Before the lecture, think about everything you have learned and discussed on the topic of artificial intelligence. What do you expect to learn more about in the lecture? Write three predictions below. Compare your predictions with a partner.

   1. _____

   2. _____

   3. _____

Follow the lecture

▷ use arrows, p. 61

2. Now follow the lecture and take notes. Remember to try to predict causes and effects.

3. **How well were you able to predict causes and effects? Circle the
statement that best describes you. Explain your answer.**

I was able to predict causes and effects _____.
a. all of the time   b. some of the time   c. none of the time   d. not sure

4. **Use your notes to answer these questions.**

1. What are the two main approaches to AI? Give examples of each.

_____

_____

_____

2. What is the Turing test? What is the Total Turing Test?

_____

_____

_____

3. What human-like skills would a machine have to have in order to pass
the Turing test?

_____

_____

_____

4. What are some of the ways that AI is currently in use?

_____

_____

_____

5. **Were you able to answer the questions in Exercise 4 using the
information in your notes? Compare your notes with a few other
students. Discuss the differences and help each other fill in any
missing information. Complete your notes.**

6. **Work with a partner and take turns. Review your notes from the
lecture. Then explain the main points of the lecture to your partner.
Talk for 2-3 minutes only.**

Discuss the Issues

Discussion Strategy

Compromise and Reach a Consensus
During group discussions, you often need to reach a consensus. In other words, you need to compromise with the other group members and come up with one idea or plan that represents the group. A compromise is something everyone can agree on, even though the individuals may disagree about some points.

Reach a compromise

1. Read the expressions for compromising and reaching a consensus. Can you add others to the list?

What's one idea we can all agree on?
What do all our ideas have in common?
So, can we all agree on . . . ?
Can you live with this?
So, it sounds like we've decided . . .

_____

_____

_____

Practice reaching a compromise

2. In groups of four, read the questions and discuss them. Keep the conversation going until every student has had a chance to practice using the language for reaching a compromise.

1. Imagine you are designing an intelligent machine for your own use. What would your machine be like? Consider these questions:

   • What would it look like?

   • What would it sound like?

   • What would it be able to do?

   • Who would use it?

   • How much would it cost?

2. What do you think is the greatest benefit and the greatest risk associated with developing intelligent machines? Use your own ideas and opinions or the ones given below. Give examples for your choices.

Possible benefits:
providing companionship or entertainment for humans
performing complicated tasks
performing dangerous tasks
performing boring tasks
assisting humans in everyday tasks
helping people learn

Possible risks:
people losing their jobs to machines
people having too much free time
people losing their privacy
people being harmed by machines

Discuss the ideas in the lecture

3. Discuss these ideas from the lecture with your classmates. Try to reach a consensus, using the phrases for compromising.

1. What are the three most significant tasks or activities that a machine could never do better than a human?

2. What are the three most significant tasks or activities currently done by humans that should be done only by machines?

3. Imagine your class is responsible for giving a grant to a scientist who is trying to develop an intelligent machine. What conditions or requirements would you attach to the money?

4. Look back at your notes. What was another idea in the lecture that you found important and interesting? Tell the class why you think it is important or interesting and ask for their opinions.

Unit Wrap-Up

1. **Go online and research an alternative or traditional medicine or treatment. Share your findings with the class. Include the following information:**

   - How long has it been used?

   - Who uses it? How popular is it?

   - What types of illnesses or injuries is it used to treat?

   - How does it work?

   - Have there been any scientific studies into its effectiveness?

2. **Think of a robot or computer from a science fiction movie or novel that you find interesting. Bring a picture of it or a passage in which it is introduced to class and describe the robot or computer to your classmates. Include the following information in your description:**

   - What is it capable of?

   - Would it pass the Turing Test?

   - Is it helpful or harmful to humans?

   - If it were possible to create such a machine today, do you think it should or should not be created? Why or why not?

3. **Read the scenario below and do the activity as a class.**

   Imagine that researchers have developed a robot doctor, which they have named Dr. Bolts. In their studies, Dr. Bolts was able to diagnose patients accurately 95% of the time. The manufacturer wants to market Dr. Bolts to community clinics and hospitals as a money-saving investment. You and your class have been hired by the manufacturer to do a focus group on community reaction to Dr. Bolts.

   - Discuss the pros and cons of Dr. Bolts. Be prepared to support your arguments.

   - For the manufacturer, come up with a list of the three best aspects and three worst aspects of using Dr. Bolts in a real clinic or hospital.

   Be sure to use the language of compromise and consensus when appropriate.

PSYCHOLOGY

psychology \saɪˈkɑlədʒi\ **The scientific study of the mind and how it influences behavior**

Chapter 7 | Sibling Relationships

CHAPTER GOALS

- Learn about sibling relationships and their possible effect on human development
- Learn a Listening Strategy: Recognize lecture language that signals comparisons and contrasts
- Learn a Note-taking Strategy: Note comparisons and contrasts
- Learn a Discussion Strategy: Expand on your own ideas during a discussion

Build Background Knowledge

Think about the topic

1. Look at the pictures. Then discuss the questions below in pairs.

1. Think about the childhoods of the children in the photos. In what ways are they probably similar? How are they different?
2. Which children do you think will grow up to be the most successful? Why?
3. What size family do you think is ideal? Why?

2. Read this newspaper article about studies done with twins to determine just how similar they really are.

Twin Studies

What determines the kind of person each of us develops into over a lifetime? How much are we influenced by our home environment, and how much are we influenced by our **genes**? One way that psychologists have tried to answer these questions is by studying twins: identical twins (coming from one fertilized egg, so sharing the same genes) and fraternal twins (coming from different eggs, so sharing 50% of their genes). By comparing these two groups, researchers hope to be able to estimate the influence of genes versus the influence of environment on the development of many human **traits**, such as personality, talents, interests, and attitudes.

Psychologists from the University of Minnesota have conducted several different studies with over 8,000 pairs of twins and their families. To determine what **accounts for** differences between twins, they have compared identical twins who were raised together with identical twins who were separated at birth and raised in different families. Their assumption is that any similarity in twins who are raised together can be **attributed to** both genes and environment, whereas similarities in twins raised apart are due only to genes, since they had different environments while growing up. Their studies indicate that genes have about a 50% influence on our personalities, while our environment accounts for the other 50%.

Researchers in this study have also tried to test the theory that we each develop a set of criteria for choosing a mate based on our genes and our **unique** experiences growing up. To do this, researchers compared the spouses of male identical twins who were raised together. They found that the spouses of these identical twins were not much more similar to each other than **random** pairs of people. They also found that two-thirds of the twins were "indifferent" to their twin's mate or "actively disliked" her. These results indicate that neither our genes nor our upbringing is a good predictor of the spouse we choose. Instead, researchers believe this choice appears to be random, and based more on whom we are near when we are ready to fall in love.

Another question this study has sought to answer is whether twins become more or less similar as they **mature**. They found that as identical twins age, they become less similar in their physical appearance, but more similar in their abilities, such as mathematical skills. On the other hand, as fraternal twins age they become less similar in these abilities.

Some psychologists are **skeptical** of twin studies. These critics question some of the assumptions made by twin researchers, such as the assumption that identical twins and fraternal twins have similar environments, or that identical twins raised apart are raised in very different environments. Some believe that, even in the same environment, there can be **disparities** in the way this environment affects siblings. As a result, it is difficult to determine clearly how much of our personality is genetically **inherited** and how much is determined by our environment.

3. Answer the questions about the article on page 69. Then discuss your answers with a partner.

  1. What do researchers hope to learn by studying twins? What have they found?

  2. To what extent do genes influence the choice of a mate? Explain.

  3. What criticisms do some researchers have of twins research?

Expand your vocabulary

4. Match the words with their definitions. Look back at the article on page 69 to check your answers.

____ **1.** gene	**a.**	to explain or give a reason for something
____ **2.** trait	**b.**	to age; to become fully grown or developed
____ **3.** account for	**c.**	difference
____ **4.** attribute to	**d.**	the biological component through which qualities are passed from parents to child
____ **5.** unique	**e.**	received from your biological parents
____ **6.** random	**f.**	doubtful that something is true or valid
____ **7.** mature	**g.**	happening or chosen by chance
____ **8.** skeptical	**h.**	a quality; part of somebody's character
____ **9.** disparity	**i.**	unlike anything else
____ **10.** inherited	**j.**	to point to as the cause of something

Discuss the reading

5. Discuss these questions in a small group. Share your answers with the class.

  1. Do you agree with the research results regarding how much of our personality comes from our genes versus our environment? Why or why not? Give some examples of people you know.

  2. How similar are you to your parents? To your siblings? What makes you unique in your family?

Review what you know

▷ p. 4

6. With a partner, write down three things in your notebook that you have learned so far about similarities among siblings.

Prepare to Listen and Take Notes

1. To help you understand the listening strategy, discuss the situation below and answer the question.

During a lecture, the professor is comparing and contrasting different things, but you can't keep track of the similarities and differences she is discussing. What could you do to keep the information straight?

Listening Strategy

Recognize Lecture Language that Signals Comparisons and Contrasts
Professors often compare and contrast different people, things, or ideas.

Listen for the words and expressions that professors use to signal similarities and differences.

Comparison lecture language

2. Read the expressions that signal comparison (similarity) and contrast (difference). Can you add others to the list?

Comparison	**Contrast**
Similarly, . . .	On the other hand, . . .
Likewise, . . .	On the contrary, . . .
In the same way/fashion, . . .	In contrast, . . .
Both X and Y . . .	Compared to X, Y is less/more . . .
Like X, Y is . . .	While/whereas X . . . , Y . . .
Also, . . .	Unlike X, Y . . .
What do X and Y have in common?	The difference between X and Y is . . .

_____   _____

_____   _____

Recognize lecture language

3. Read the excerpt from a lecture on twins. Underline and label the lecture language that signals comparison or contrast.

. . . .

Twins occur in about 1 in 85 births. The two types of twins are fraternal, . . . or dizygotic, . . . and identical, . . . or monozygotic. The difference between the two types comes from a difference in how they begin life. While fraternal twins come from the fertilization of two separate eggs, identical twins come from a single fertilized egg that later splits in two.

There are many stories of twins separated at birth who turn out to be amazingly similar. For example, Barbara Herbert and Daphne Goodship were identical twins who were given up for adoption into different families at birth. When they met at the age of 40, they discovered that they both worked in local government, met their husbands at a town dance at the age of 16, and both had given birth to two boys and a girl. Like Barbara, Daphne dyed her hair auburn and drank her coffee cold.

. . . .

4. Listen to an excerpt from a lecture on sibling relationships about Bill Clinton and his brother Roger Clinton. Match the first part of each sentence with the correct second part.

_____ **1.** Bill and Roger Clinton   **a.** struggled to develop a career.

_____ **2.** Both Bill and Roger   **b.** had different biological fathers.

_____ **3.** One was ambitious, the other   **c.** were close to their mother.

5. Listen to the excerpt again. As you listen, write down at least four instances of lecture language that signals comparison or contrast. Then listen once more and write down what is being compared or contrasted. Circle the correct label.

1. Lecture language: _____

Compared/contrasted: _____

_____

2. Lecture language: _____

Compared/contrasted: _____

_____

3. Lecture language: _____

Compared/contrasted: _____

_____

4. Lecture language: _____

Compared/contrasted: _____

_____

Note-taking Strategy

Note Comparisons and Contrasts
When taking notes about ideas in a lecture that are being compared and contrasted, it's often easier to put your notes into a list or chart. This way you can easily see how the items are similar or different. You can organize your notes by listing the similarities and differences for each item, or by listing each point to be compared and contrasted.

6. With a partner, look at two students' notes from the lecture about Bill and Roger Clinton. Which system do you prefer? Why?

Bill Clinton	Roger Clinton
- born 1946	- born 1956
- father died before born	- father Roger Clinton
- mother married Roger Clinton age 4	
- difficult childhood	- " "
- close to brother, mother	- " "
- good student	- drug problems; dropped out of college
- successful politician	- arrested, unsuccessful music career

	Bill Clinton	Roger Clinton
childhood	born 1946	" 1956
	father died	" father
	Abusive step-father	
school	Excellent student	Dropped out of college
	Yale Law School	
career	Gov of AK	Arrested for selling drugs
	U.S. Pres.	Played in rock bands; many jobs
		Not much of a career

7. Work with a partner. Take turns reading this excerpt aloud. While one of you reads, the other takes notes using a list or chart. Then switch roles. When you are finished, compare your notes.

. . . .

Both Joe Kennedy and his brother John were born into privilege—a wealthy family in Boston. They grew up as the two oldest siblings in a family of nine children. But in most other ways they were quite different. Joe, the first-born son, was favored by his parents. He excelled academically and aspired to be President. John, on the other hand, was a sickly child and mediocre student. Like his brother Joe, John fought in World War II. John escaped with minor injuries, while Joe was killed when his plane was shot down.

. . . .

Listen and Take Notes

Make predictions

▷ p. 8

1. Before the lecture, think about everything you have learned and discussed on the topic of sibling relationships. What do you expect to learn more about in the lecture? Write three predictions below. Compare your predictions with a partner.

1. _____

2. _____

3. _____

Follow the lecture

▷ compare/contrast, p. 73

2. Now follow the lecture and take notes, using a chart or list. Remember to listen for the lecture language that signals comparisons and contrasts.

Chapter 7 Sibling Relationships

3. How well were you able to recognize the lecture language? Circle the statement that best describes you. Explain your answer.

I was able to recognize the lecture language for comparison and contrast _____.
a. all of the time   **b.** some of the time   **c.** none of the time   **d.** not sure

4. Use your notes to answer these questions.

1. Which siblings tend to be the most successful? The least successful?

_____

_____

_____

2. What have researchers found to be generally true of middle children?

_____

_____

_____

3. What are at least three ways that birth order can help to explain disparities between siblings?

_____

_____

_____

4. What are at least three other reasons for these disparities?

_____

_____

_____

5. Were you able to answer the questions in Exercise 4 using the information in your notes? Compare your notes with a few other students. Discuss the differences and help each other fill in any missing information. Complete your notes.

6. Work with a partner and take turns. Review your notes from the lecture. Then explain the main points of the lecture to your partner. Talk for 2-3 minutes only.

Discuss the Issues

Discussion Strategy

Expand on Your Own Ideas
Sometimes during a group or class discussion, you may think of something else you would like to say after your turn has passed. There are certain phrases you can use that will help you to go back to your original idea and expand on it.

Expand on your own ideas

1. Read the expressions for expanding on your own ideas. Can you add others to the list?

What I meant before was . . .
I'd like to go back to what I was saying earlier . . .
Let me add something to what I said before . . .
What I was trying to say was . . .
About my earlier point, . . .
About what I said earlier, . . .
I'd like to take my earlier point a step further . . .

_____

_____

_____

Practice expanding on your idea

2. In groups of four, read the questions and discuss them. Start your discussion with more general ideas so that you can expand on them during the discussion. Keep the conversation going until every student has had a chance to practice using the target language. Use your own ideas and opinions or the ones given below.

1. How would you describe the ideal family? Think about the following aspects of a family:

> family size
> sibling relationships
> parent/child relationships
> roles and responsibilities of family members
> time spent together
> role of grandparents and other extended family members
> household income level
> physical location (house/apartment, city/small town/country)
> shared or separate bedrooms

2. Would you like to be a twin? Why or why not?

Discuss the ideas in the lecture

3. Discuss these ideas from the lecture with your classmates. Remember to use the phrases for expanding on your own ideas.

1. What is your birth order in your family? Has birth order influenced the siblings in your family as described in the lecture? In what ways?

2. In your experience, are oldest and only siblings most successful? Are there any characteristics of oldest, middle, or youngest siblings not mentioned in the lecture that you have noticed? How about only children?

3. Think about your closest friends from different times of your life. Do they tend to be of one birth-order category or from different categories? Why do think this is? What might it say about you?

4. Look back at your notes. What was another idea in the lecture that you found important and interesting? Tell the class why you think it is important or interesting, and ask for their opinions.

Chapter 8 | Multiple Intelligences

CHAPTER GOALS | • Learn about intelligence tests and the theory of multiple intelligences
• Learn a Listening Strategy: Recognize non-verbal signals that indicate when information is important
• Learn a Note-taking Strategy: Use numbered lists to organize information
• Learn a Discussion Strategy: Keep the discussion on topic

Build Background Knowledge

Think about the topic

1. Look at the pictures. Then discuss the questions below in pairs.

1. What sorts of skills are these children learning from their various activities?

2. How will each of those skills help them in their adult lives?

3. Which children appear more intelligent? Why?

2. Read this article from a parenting magazine presenting some of the controversy around intelligence tests for children.

Intelligence Tests

During childhood, the most commonly used **aptitude** tests are intelligence tests, or IQ tests. "IQ" is actually an abbreviation for "intelligence quotient." Originally, IQ scores were calculated as a quotient: the age at which most children achieve a particular score on the test, divided by the child's actual age, multiplied by 100. The calculation of IQ scores is designed so that the results produce a *bell curve*—most students scoring in the middle range and a few scoring at the upper and lower ends of the scale. When these results are put into graph form, the shape resembles a bell.

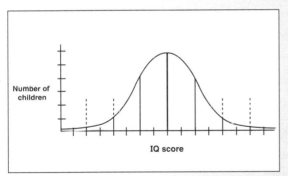

Graph showing a bell curve.

Two common intelligence tests are the Stanford-Binet and the Wechsler intelligence tests. Both **assess** several **capabilities**, including general knowledge, reasoning ability, mathematical skill, memory, and vocabulary. They also assess **spatial** perception, such as the ability to put together a puzzle or arrange colored blocks to match a specific **pattern**.

IQ tests are reliable in predicting a child's success in school, but many psychologists caution against relying too heavily on these scores as a measure of a child's capabilities. In fact, some critics **dispute** the validity of using IQ tests at all, citing many factors that can affect a child's ability to perform well on them.

First of all, critics point out that children develop at different rates, depending on their biology, family, school, and environment. They also state that performance on an IQ test **reflects** not just a child's aptitude for learning, but also his or her already acquired knowledge: vocabulary, math, as well as cultural knowledge that is learned, not inborn. Performance on IQ tests also reflects the ability to focus and pay attention, so children who have attention problems may be at a disadvantage. Moreover, a child's performance can be affected by illness or emotional stress.

Some educators argue that all of these factors should be considered when analyzing the scores of individual children, so as not to underestimate the intelligence of children with disadvantages. Not doing so could create a false assessment of a child's true intellectual capacity and negatively affect his or her motivation to learn.

One final criticism of IQ tests is that they view intelligence in much too narrow a way, by looking at intelligence as one **entity**, measurable by one test. Success in life, especially in different cultures, may be more dependent on other **distinct** capabilities and talents that are not included in intelligence tests. For this reason, educators and psychologists encourage parents not to see an IQ score as a sure indicator of their child's future success.

3. Answer the questions about the article on page 79. Then discuss your answers with a partner.

1. What is a bell curve? How do intelligence tests follow the bell curve?

2. What abilities are IQ tests designed to measure?

3. What are some criticisms of IQ tests?

Expand your vocabulary

4. Match the words with their definitions. Look back at the article on page 79 to check your answers.

____ **1.** aptitude   **a.** to argue against something official or scientific

____ **2.** assess   **b.** the quality of being able to do something

____ **3.** capability   **c.** clearly different

____ **4.** spatial   **d.** to judge or form an opinion about something

____ **5.** pattern   **e.** to show or represent something

____ **6.** dispute   **f.** relating to the size or position of something

____ **7.** reflect   **g.** something that has its own separate identity

____ **8.** entity   **h.** the innate or inborn potential to learn

____ **9.** distinct   **i.** a regularly repeated arrangement

Discuss the reading

5. Discuss these questions in a small group. Share your answers with the class.

1. How might a child's background affect his or her ability to perform well on an intelligence test? Give some examples.

2. What are some other human capabilities that are not reflected in IQ tests?

Review what you know

▷ p. 4

6. With a partner, write down three things in your notebook that you have learned so far about measuring intelligence.

Prepare to Listen and Take Notes

1. To help you understand the listening strategy, discuss the situation below and answer the questions.

You notice that the professor often uses gestures or facial expressions when emphasizing key information. What kinds of non-verbal signals do English speakers typically use? How could these non-verbal signals help you follow the lecture and take notes better?

Recognize Non-Verbal Signals for Important Information
There are some common non-verbal signals that English speakers use to signal or emphasize important concepts or information. Being aware of these signals can help you to identify ideas that the professor wishes to emphasize.

Watch for non-verbal signals that indicate key ideas and information and write them down.

Non-verbal signals

2. Read the list of non-verbal signals for indicating that something is important. Can you add others to the list?

The professor writes or points to information on the board.
The professor writes or presents something as a projection.
The professor pauses and looks at students intently or moves toward students.
The professor uses gestures:
- emphasizes or symbolizes an action or an idea with his/her hands
- counts out points on his/her fingers
- makes quotation marks in the air to emphasize or show ironic use of words
- compares and contrasts two different concepts with his/her hands

_____

_____

Recognize non-verbal signals

3. Look at the photos of a professor giving a lecture. Then read the quotes below. Match the non-verbal signal with the idea the professor is expressing.

1.  2.

3.  4.

____ **a.** "IQ tests can help schools assess student needs. On the other hand,…"

____ **b.** "So, when we say a person is "smart," what do we really mean?"

____ **c.** "The tests used today are the Stanford-Binet and the Wechsler."

____ **d.** "Today I'll discuss three different perspectives of IQ tests."

4. Listen to this short lecture on measuring intelligence in adults. Then write T for True or F for False next to each statement.

_____ **1.** General intelligence is defined as one entity, one certain level of ability.

_____ **2.** Fluid intelligence refers to a person's general knowledge of facts and information.

_____ **3.** Crystallized intelligence is the ability to reason and analyze.

_____ **4.** Fluid intelligence decreases over time, while crystallized intelligence increases.

5. Now follow the short lecture. As you watch, write down the non-verbal signals that the speaker uses to indicate important ideas. Watch again and write down the ideas.

1. Non-verbal signal: _____

Important idea: _____

2. Non-verbal signal: _____

Important idea: _____

3. Non-verbal signal: _____

Important idea: _____

4. Non-verbal signal: _____

Important idea: _____

5. Non-verbal signal: _____

Important idea: _____

6. Non-verbal signal: _____

Important idea: _____

Use Numbered Lists to Organize Information
Professors will often present lists of ideas or related items that you will need to remember. In this case, it's helpful to write down the information in the form of a list, using indents to signify relationships between ideas.

Use numbered lists

6. Look at a section of one student's notes on the short lecture about measuring intelligence. Discuss with a partner how the student has shown the relationship between pieces of information.

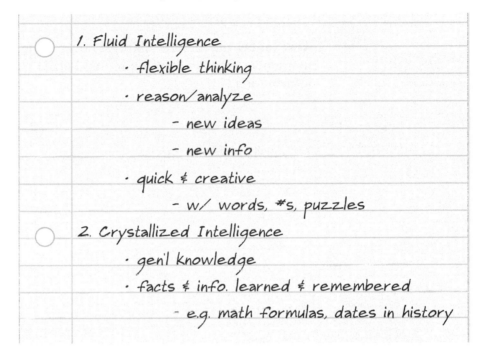

1. Fluid Intelligence
   · flexible thinking
   · reason/analyze
      - new ideas
      - new info
   · quick & creative
      - w/ words, #s, puzzles
2. Crystallized Intelligence
   · gen'l knowledge
   · facts & info. learned & remembered
      - e.g. math formulas, dates in history

7. Work with a partner. Take turns reading aloud this excerpt from a lecture on Sternberg's three forms of intelligence. While one of you reads, the other takes notes using a numbered list. Then switch roles. When you are finished, compare your notes.

Robert Sternberg has proposed that intelligence can be divided into three categories. These are analytic intelligence, creative intelligence, and practical intelligence. Analytic intelligence refers to the ability to learn, remember, and think efficiently. This includes the ability to plan, to pay attention, to process information, and use verbal and logical skills. The second kind of intelligence is creative intelligence. Creative intelligence reflects the ability to be flexible and innovative in new situations. It allows people to find new and unusual solutions to problems and tasks. The third intelligence—practical intelligence—refers to a person's ability to adapt to new situations and solve "real-world" problems, such as how to manage a home or career, and meet the needs of families, neighbors, and colleagues. Some people might refer to this type of intelligence as "street smarts" rather than "book smarts."

Listen and Take Notes

Make predictions

1. Before the lecture, think about everything you have read and discussed on the topic of intelligence. What do you expect to learn more about in the lecture? Write three predictions below. Compare your predictions with a partner.

   1. _____

   2. _____

   3. _____

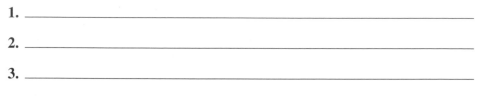

Follow the lecture

▷ numbered lists, p. 83

2. Now follow the lecture and take notes using a numbered list. Remember to pay attention to non-verbal signals for important information.

3. **How well were you able to recognize the non-verbal signals of importance? Check the statement that best describes you. Explain your answer.**

_____ I was able to recognize when the professor was using a non-verbal signal and it helped me catch important information.

_____ I was able to recognize the non-verbal signals, but I wasn't always able to connect those to the information the professor was giving.

_____ I'm not sure that I was always able to recognize the non-verbal signals or the way they connected to important information.

4. **Use your notes to answer these questions.**

1. What are Gardner's seven types of intelligence? Describe them.

_____

_____

_____

_____

_____

_____

2. What are the criticisms of the theory of multiple intelligences?

_____

_____

_____

3. How have many educators found this theory useful?

_____

_____

5. **Were you able to answer the questions in Exercise 4 using the information in your notes? Compare your notes with a few other students. Discuss the differences and help each other fill in any missing information. Complete your notes.**

6. **Work with a partner and take turns. Review your notes from the lecture. Then explain the main points of the lecture to your partner. Talk for 2-3 minutes only.**

Discuss the Issues

Discussion Strategy

Keep the Discussion on Topic
During a discussion, students sometimes get off topic—they bring up ideas that aren't related to the discussion topic. In this situation, the other students should politely try to bring the discussion back to the original topic; otherwise, you may not be able to reach any conclusions or complete the assigned task. Use expressions to keep the discussion focused and on topic.

Stay on topic

1. Read the expressions for bringing a discussion back on topic and keeping a discussion focused. Can you add others to the list?

I think maybe we're getting off the topic/subject.
I think we're getting off track.
Can we go back to _____?
Maybe we should get back to the question.
Let's get back to . . .
Maybe we could talk about that later, but for now I think we should…
That's a good point, but . . .
Let's remember our purpose here. . . .
Let's stay focused.

_____

_____

_____

_____

Practice staying on topic

2. In groups of four, read the situations and discuss them. Keep the conversation going until everyone has had a chance to practice using the target language. Be sure to stray from the topic sometimes so you can practice bringing the discussion back on topic.

1. Of the seven types of intelligence in Gardner's theory of multiple intelligences, which is the most important for the average high-school student? The average college student? The average adult in the work world? A parent?

> linguistic
> logical-mathematical
> spatial
> musical
> bodily-kinesthetic
> interpersonal
> intrapersonal

2. When you consider all seven types of intelligences in Gardner's theory, who do you think are more intelligent—men or women? Why? Support your opinion with examples.

Discuss the ideas in the lecture

3. Discuss these ideas from the lecture with your classmates. Remember to use the phrases for keeping the discussion on topic.

1. How do you define intelligence? Do you think the skills measured by IQ tests are an accurate or adequate measure of intelligence?

2. Which of the multiple intelligences do you think you possess? Which do you not possess or have less of? Give some examples.

3. Do you agree with any of the criticisms of the theory of multiple intelligences? If so, which ones? Why? If not, why not? Should teachers consider this theory when teaching and assessing their students?

4. Look back at your notes. What was another idea in the lecture that you found important and interesting? Tell the class why you think it is important or interesting and ask for their opinions.

Unit Wrap-Up

1. Research a famous person with a high IQ. How high is this person's IQ? What did this person accomplish? What different types of intelligence do you think this person has/had? Write a brief report and present it in a small group. Be prepared to ask and answer questions.

2. Go online and find a multiple intelligence test. Take the test and discuss your results with a partner. Did any of the results surprise you? Why or why not? Which types of intelligence do you think are the most common? Which are the most unusual? Why do you think so?

3. Interview two or three siblings from another family separately. Find out about their personal characteristics, such as their strengths, interests, and accomplishments.

   - Ask each sibling about himself or herself, and also ask each about the others.

   - Make a chart in which you plot your results.

   - Analyze the results and draw some conclusions. In what ways are the siblings similar? How are they different? Do they have the characteristics related to birth order that you learned about in Chapter 7? What do you think explains their differences?

   - Discuss your results with a partner or in a small group.

   Notes: _____

   _____

   _____

   _____

   _____

   _____

   _____

   _____

ART & DESIGN

art \ɑrt\ The use of the imagination to express ideas or feelings

design \dɪˈzaɪn\ The arrangement of lines, shapes, and colors for aesthetic effect

Chapter 9 | The Art of Graffiti

CHAPTER GOALS

- Learn about graffiti art and artist Keith Haring
- Learn a Listening Strategy: Recognize lecture language that signals a definition
- Review and practice all note-taking strategies
- Learn a Discussion Strategy: Indicate to others when you are preparing to speak or pausing to collect your thoughts before continuing

Build Background Knowledge

Think about the topic

1. Look at the picture of graffiti. Then discuss the questions below in pairs.

1. How common is this type of graffiti in your neighborhood or city? Do you see more or less of it these days?
2. What do you think of graffiti? Do you see it as art? Does it have a mostly positive or mostly negative effect on the appearance of buildings and the community? Why do you think so?

2. Read this discussion from an online art history class.

File   Edit   View   Tools   Help

◄ Back   ► Forward   ⊗ Stop   ⇄ Refresh   🏠 Home

VANDALISM OR ART?

Professor Lind: Graffiti is **controversial.** Some people like it; some people don't, but is it art? Your thoughts . . . ?

MARCO: *I think graffiti on buildings is mostly ugly; it's an **eyesore.** I don't know why people think they should be able to draw and write anywhere they want to. Why should we have to look at it? Graffiti looks like garbage and makes the area look like nobody's taking care of it.*

Professor Lind: So something must be pretty in order to be considered art?

MARCO: *No, it's not that. It takes some artistic talent to make some graffiti, but basically it's an act of **vandalism.** I believe that graffiti is not art. If you write or paint on someone else's property without his **permission,** you are breaking the law. That might be a political statement, but we shouldn't call it art. If we call it art, we are saying that it's okay to damage other people's property.*

Jesse: That's a good point, but I still think graffiti is art. It is the creative **expression** of the graffiti artist. How can we draw that kind of **boundary** and say graffiti can't be art just because it's created without permission?

Shannon: Regarding graffiti's effect on the appearance of the community, I think it's mostly a positive one. It can make ugly gray walls and buildings more colorful and beautiful.

MARCO: *But not for long. Graffiti may not be **permanent,** but it costs a lot of money for people and cities to remove it. Usually they don't, and it just gets old and dirty and even uglier.*

Professor Lind: Let's get back to the subject. Shannon, you think graffiti IS art?

Shannon: Not all graffiti. I think people who just write a name or some profanity—well, that's just vandalism.

MARCO: *Exactly! I agree. It's vandalism.*

Lee: But every day I look at ads of all kinds in my neighborhood—posters, billboards, signs in windows. They are just as colorful and wild as the graffiti. These legal images and ideas are very much a part of our view of the world every single day, but for some reason people don't think of them as ugly. Creating graffiti is a way to take more control of the public space.

Jesse: I agree. The ideas and messages in graffiti can act as a response to the commercial messages. The messages in graffiti have more **integrity** because they aren't just trying to sell you something; they are pictures and messages from people in my community. The artists are trying to **engage** with each other, and with me. I can understand why graffiti artists want to create their own visuals in their own neighborhood.

Professor Lind: Okay, very good. Let's move on now, and talk about the politics of graffiti . . .

3. Answer the questions about the reading on page 91. Then discuss your answers with a partner.

1. Which students think that graffiti is not, or is not always, art? What are their reasons?

2. Which students believe that graffiti is or can be art? What are their reasons?

4. Match the words with their definitions. Look back at the reading on page 91 to check your answers.

____ **1.** controversial   **a.** lasting for a long time or forever

____ **2.** vandalism   **b.** putting feelings or thoughts into words or actions

____ **3.** permission   **c.** causing public discussion and disagreement

____ **4.** expression   **d.** the act of allowing somebody to do something

____ **5.** boundary   **e.** to connect with someone emotionally

____ **6.** permanent   **f.** the quality of being honest and having firm moral ideas

____ **7.** integrity   **g.** damaging property on purpose

____ **8.** engage   **h.** the line that marks the limits of something

5. Circle the phrase with a similar meaning to the underlined word.

All the garbage on the street is an <u>eyesore</u> in the community.
a. something that is unpleasant to look at
b. something that is uncommon
c. something that is special or unique

6. Discuss these questions in a small group. Share your answers with the class.

1. Which student in the discussion do you agree with most closely? Explain why you agree with that student.

2. Do you think that graffiti and advertising have the same effect on the appearance of a community? Should there be stronger laws to limit graffiti? Should there be stronger laws to limit advertising?

▷ p. 4

7. With a partner, write down three things in your notebook that you have learned so far about graffiti.

Prepare to Listen and Take Notes

Recognize Lecture Language that Signals a Definition
Professors often use new words or familiar words and phrases that have a different meaning in the subject area. When professors use these words for the first time, they usually also define them. It is important to catch the definition the first time, because they may start to use them regularly and not define them again.

Listen for the words and expressions that professors use to signal a definition.

Definition lecture language

1. Read the expressions that signal a definition. Can you add others to the list?

The term for this is X.   X means _____.
This is called X. Now, X refers to . . .   X is the term for _____.
What I mean by X is . . .   _____, or what some call X, . . .
What I mean when I say X is . . .   X, or _____, . . .
What do I mean by X? Well, . . .   X, meaning . . .
What is X? X is . . .

_____

_____

Recognize lecture language

2. Read the excerpts from a lecture about subway graffiti. Circle the word(s) that is being defined. Underline and label the lecture language that signals the definition and also the definition.

Excerpt 1
In the subways of New York in the early 1970s, writers, . . . what I mean by writers is graffiti artists, . . . started doing something new. They started to tag their work. Tag is the term for a writer's signature. Before then, no one focused on who was making the graffiti. A New York writer named Taki 183, . . . Taki 183 was his pseudonym, meaning the nickname he chose to sign his work, . . . he was the first to get fame and media attention for tagging trains. He traveled all over New York and tagged everywhere.

Excerpt 2
Pop Art was a big influence on artist Keith Haring. Pop Art is the term we use for the style of art created by artists like Andy Warhol, artists who used themes and techniques taken from mass culture. What do I mean when I say mass culture? I mean things like advertising, popular movies, fashion magazines, comic books, . . . things like that. Pop Art used popular culture as a guide instead of the culture of the "high art" world. In this way, it was able to engage a much larger public.

3. Listen to the lecture about New York style graffiti. Then write T for true or F for false next to each statement.

____ 1. "New York style" graffiti is only found in New York.

____ 2. Subway writers have one main goal: to tag as many subway cars as they can.

____ 3. The general public liked the graffiti and saw it as a new art form.

4. Listen to the lecture again. As you listen, write down the lecture language that signals a definition for the words and terms below. Then listen once more and write down the definition.

1. Word: genre

Lecture language: _____

Definition: _____

_____

2. Term: "get up"

Lecture language: _____

Definition: _____

_____

3. Term: "making a burner"

Lecture language: _____

Definition: _____

_____

4. Word: contradictory

Lecture language: _____

Definition: _____

_____

5. Term: "buffing"

Lecture language: _____

Definition: _____

_____

Review note-taking
strategies

5. Read the transcript from a lecture on integrity and the graffiti artist. Then, look at one student's notes from the lecture, which are incomplete. Think about the note-taking strategies you have learned. Complete the notes. Compare your work with a partner.

. . . .

In the graffiti art world, there are differences of opinion about what gives a writer integrity. Some people believe that to have integrity on the street the artist must stay outside the formal art world and make no money from his work. For example, Revs, a graffiti artist, believes as soon as money is involved, the artist loses integrity. He became well known in New York City in the early 1990s for his writing and he has never revealed his true name to the public. He now makes sculptures and asks permission to put them up, . . . but he never takes money for his work.

But many graffiti artists think it's okay to also earn a living from art. San Francisco artist Barry McGee is a contemporary artist . . . and his art appears both on the street and in museums and galleries around the world. He sees no conflict with doing both. Barry started creating graffiti art on the streets of San Francisco when he was a teenager using the nickname "Twist." This led to studying art formally at the San Francisco Art Institute, . . . and then he also started creating art in galleries and museums. In fact, in 2001 he was chosen to exhibit some of his work at the Venice Biennale International Art Exhibition—an important exhibition of contemporary artists from all over the world. He sees the two kinds of art he creates as being very different. He would definitely agree with Revs that the art he creates for galleries, . . . well, that it's quite different from the street art he does. Although his gallery work is strongly influenced by graffiti writing and street culture, he doesn't see it as graffiti.

. . . .

Integrity: graffiti art

2 artists

Revs

$ ⟶   Makes money as an artist

                                Street art + gallery/

                                museum art

Only uses street name

                                Street art ≠ gallery art

Listen and Take Notes

Make predictions

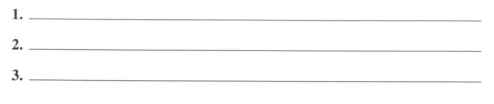 p. 8

1. Before the lecture, think about everything you have read and discussed on the topic of graffiti. What do you expect to learn more about in the lecture? Write down three predictions below. Compare your predictions with a partner.

1. _____

2. _____

3. _____

Follow the lecture

2. Now follow the lecture and take notes using the note-taking strategies you have learned. Remember to listen for the lecture language that signals definitions.

3. **How well were you able to recognize the lecture language? Check the statement that best describes you. Explain your answer.**

I was able to recognize the lecture language for definitions _____.
a. all of the time   **b.** some of the time   **c.** none of the time   **d.** not sure

4. **Use your notes to answer these questions.**

   1. Why does New York City remove graffiti?

   _____

   _____

   _____

   2. What are semiotics and how did Keith Haring use semiotics in his art?

   _____

   _____

   _____

   3. What are three characteristics of Keith Haring's artwork?

   _____

   _____

   _____

   4. Why did some people in the art world criticize Keith Haring for opening the Pop Shop?

   _____

   _____

   _____

5. **Were you able to answer the questions in Exercise 4 using the information in your notes? Compare your notes with a few other students. Discuss the differences and help each other fill in any missing information. Complete your notes.**

6. **Work with a partner and take turns. Review your notes from the lecture. Then explain the main points of the lecture to your partner. Talk for 2-3 minutes only.**

Discuss the Issues

Discussion Strategy

Pause and Collect Your Thoughts
Sometimes you might need a little extra time to think and find the words you need to express your ideas. Other times, you want to pause before continuing, but you don't want others to think you're finished speaking. Use expressions and verbal signals to let others know you are preparing to speak or that you need a moment to collect your thoughts.

Pause and collect your thoughts

1. Read the expressions that indicate to listeners when you need a moment to think or are preparing to speak. Can you add others to the list?

Pausing before continuing your thoughts
These "expressions" keep the focus on you while you pause in the middle of a thought or before you move to another point.

Well, . . .   _____
Hmmm . . .
Ummm, . . .   _____
Let's see, . . .
Okay, . . .   _____
So, . . .
Yes, yes, . . .   _____

Collecting your thoughts
These expressions can "buy time" while you put your thoughts together. Say them slowly while you organize your thoughts and prepare to speak. Speakers often combine these expressions with one of the pausing expressions above.

That's a good question.
That's an interesting point.
Let me think about that for a moment.
I'm not sure what to think.

_____

_____

_____

Practice collecting your thoughts

2. In groups of four, read the questions and discuss them, making sure to ask each other questions during the discussion. Keep the conversation going until every student has had a chance to practice pausing and collecting his or her thoughts.

1. Do you like the work of artists like Keith Haring? Explain your answer.

2. Do you think graffiti is or can be art? Explain your answer.

3. If your school or community were given an original Keith Haring painting, where and in what way do you think it should be displayed?

Discuss the ideas in the lecture

3. Discuss these ideas from the lecture with your classmates. Remember to use the phrases for pausing or collecting your thoughts when you need to.

1. New York City spends several million dollars a year to remove graffiti from its subways and streets. Is that money well spent? What do you think would be the result if the graffiti were not removed? How might people react? How might graffiti writers react?

2. Some people think Keith Haring "sold out" because he created artwork for advertising and he put artwork on products like t-shirts and postcards in the Pop Shop. Haring said that he just wanted his artwork to reach and engage the general public. What do you think? Was he more interested in making money or reaching a bigger audience? Do you think artists lose their integrity when they sell their work or use it to make money in other ways?

3. Graffiti has been called a "bottom up" form of art, meaning that it got its start with the public and then rose up to the art world, rather than a "top down" art form, meaning art that is created in an established way and then delivered to the public. What other art forms could be called "bottom up" today? What do you think of them? Is one way better than another? Why or why not?

4. Look back at your notes. What was another idea in the lecture that you found important and interesting? Tell the class why you think it is important or interesting and ask for their opinions.

Chapter 10 | Design Basics

CHAPTER GOALS

- Learn about the basic concepts of interior design
- Learn a Listening Strategy: Recognize lecture language that signals citations—paraphrases and quotations
- Review and practice all note-taking strategies
- Learn a Discussion Strategy: Support your ideas by paraphrasing and quoting others in a discussion

Build Background Knowledge

Think about the topic

1. Look at the pictures. Then discuss the questions below in pairs.

1. In what ways are these two rooms similar? In what ways are they different? Which do you prefer? Why?

2. Think of a room that you enjoy being in. Describe what it looks like and what activities you like to do there. Why is this room good for this type of activity?

Design Basics—Line

In geometry, a line is defined as the connection between two points. In interior design, we look at shapes of furniture and design elements and think about the lines they create. Staircases and window designs are excellent places to study the effects of line.

To create an environment with pleasing aesthetics, line is one of the most important elements to consider. Usually different types of lines will be found in every room, but one type of line will be dominant to create overall harmony in a space. Rooms adjacent to each other may use line differently to add character. In general, people find one type of line more aesthetically pleasing than the others. The most important consideration, however, is whether the dominant line type is compatible with how the room will be used. Consider these types of lines and their effects.

Horizontals: This type of line feels stable and secure. It feels in harmony with the earth because we associate horizontal lines with the horizon. They can make a room look wider or longer than it really is. Too many horizontal lines, however, can make a room appear overly calm and restful, and even boring. Horizontal lines help make smooth and subtle transitions between rooms.

Verticals: Like horizontal lines, vertical lines feel stable, but they can also make a room seem taller than it is. The eye is drawn upward to look up to the ceiling or sky. Tall vertical lines have a strong psychological impact. They make us fell smaller and in the presence of something important. For this reason, they are often used in government buildings, such as courthouses and town halls. Vertical lines create a formal environment, but if not used appropriately, the formality can feel confining and people will respond negatively.

Diagonals: Diagonal lines give the impression of movement. They make a room more dynamic. This is because we associate these lines with action. Diagonal lines are stimulating, but too many of them may be overstimulating and cause people to feel uncomfortable and nervous.

3. Answer the questions about the reading on page 101. Then discuss your answers with a partner.

1. What creates the lines we see in a room?

2. What are the positive effects of each type of line?

3. What are the possible negative effects of each type of line?

4. Match the words with their definitions. Look back at the reading on page 101 to check your answers.

____ **1.** aesthetics	**a.** to react emotionally to something
____ **2.** dominant	**b.** able to create excitement or interest
____ **3.** compatible	**c.** the strongest or most important
____ **4.** harmony	**d.** a pleasant combination of things
____ **5.** subtle	**e.** suitable to be used together
____ **6.** impact	**f.** not very noticeable, not strong or bright
____ **7.** respond	**g.** the effect or impression created by something
____ **8.** dynamic	**h.** full of energy; associated with movement
____ **9.** stimulating	**i.** qualities of beauty

5. Circle the phrase with a similar meaning to the underlined phrase.

My sister's apartment is all black, white, and red. The strong contrast is not
aesthetically pleasing to me, but she thinks it's fun and dynamic.

a. beautiful to look at   **b.** boring to look at   **c.** funny to look at

6. Discuss these questions in a small group. Share your answers with the class.

1. Look at the room you are in now. What kind of line is used the most? What effect does it have on the room? Are these lines typical of this sort of room? Why do you think so?

2. Think again about the room you enjoy being in (the room you chose to talk about in Exercise 2 on page 100). What kind of line is dominant in that room? What impact do the lines have?

7. With a partner, write down three things in your notebook that you have learned so far about design.

▷ p. 4

Prepare to Listen and Take Notes

1. To help you understand the listening strategy, discuss the situation below and answer the question.

The reading list for your class includes several different books and magazines. The professor often refers to information or ideas in the reading material that you would like to learn more about. How can you figure out where to find the information in the reading list?

Listening Strategy

Recognize Lecture Language for Citing Information
In a lecture, a professor will sometimes support ideas by giving, or *citing*, the source of a piece of information. This is usually done by quoting or paraphrasing another person, such as an expert in the field.

Listen for the language that professors use to signal that they are using someone else's words or ideas to support the information in the lecture. Make a note of the source in case you need it later.

Citation lecture language

2. Read the expressions that signal when a professor is citing another source of information. Can you add others to the list?

Paraphrasing (not exact words)
[Source] states/says/suggests/
   argues/believes that . . .
In [title], [source] says/states/
   suggests/argues . . .
According to [source], . . .
To paraphrase [source], . . .

Quoting (exact words)
[Source] says, and I quote, "_____."
[Source] said, quote, "_____."
In the words of [source], "_____."
To quote [source], "_____."
This is what [source] calls "_____."

_____   _____

_____   _____

Recognize lecture language

3. Read the excerpt from a lecture about color in design. Underline and label the lecture language that cites the source of a quotation (Q) or a paraphrase (P).

. . . .

When designing a room, you want to be sure that it is not overstimulating or understimulating. In the book *Color and Light in Man-Made Environments*, Mahnke says that you need to have some sameness in color, shapes, line, etc., but you also need some variety. According to Mahnke, overstimulation can cause physical stress—for example, increased breathing rate, heart rate, and muscle tension. But understimulation can also be a problem. He states that people in understimulating environments often feel restless, have trouble concentrating, and feel irritated. However, as color researcher Faber Birren says, and I quote, "people expect all of their senses to be moderately stimulated at all times." He believes that this is because this constant moderate stimulation is what is present in nature.

. . . .

4. Listen to an excerpt from a lecture on the impact of color choice in rooms. Match the item on the left with its description on the right.

____ **1.** blue   **a.** a "safe" color

____ **2.** white   **b.** a warm color

____ **3.** red   **c.** a cool color

5. Listen to the excerpt again. As you listen, write down the lecture language that signals a paraphrase or quotation. Circle the correct label. Then listen once more and write down the main idea of the paraphrase or quotation.

1. Lecture language: _____

Paraphrase/quotation

Main idea:_____

_____

2. Lecture language: _____

Paraphrase/quotation

Main idea:_____

_____

3. Lecture language: _____

Paraphrase/quotation

Main idea:_____

_____

4. Lecture language: _____

Paraphrase/quotation

Main idea:_____

_____

Note-taking Strategy

Review
Review all the note-taking strategies that you have learned in this book.

6. Read the transcript from a lecture on the effects of color in interior space. Then look at one student's notes from the lecture. Identify which note-taking strategies the student has used and write them in your notebook. Give at least one example for each strategy.

Today I'm going to review some of the ideas we've discussed regarding the placement of color in a room. The location of the color—whether it's on the floor or the walls or the ceiling—can create quite different effects, . . . um, . . . psychologically. FIrst, let's talk about two colors commonly used indoors and how they can have very different impacts depending on their location.

Yellow is a color that can be used quite effectively indoors. Depending on how dark or light it is, it can create a positive, . . . a happy atmosphere. A light yellow on the ceiling can make a room glow and can create stimulating energy. On the walls, if not too bright, it can also be stimulating and add light, . . . because it actually appears brighter than white. Used on the floor, however, yellow can be very distracting and irritating. I mean, how many times have you seen yellow on the floor? Ever? Probably not. This is something people feel intuitively, . . . that yellow is better for the walls and ceiling than the floor.

Now, green is almost the opposite. It's a much better color for the floor than the ceiling. A natural shade of green on the floor or on walls . . . it's usually soothing and relaxing. In Wilkens' words, "green walls or carpeting can create a good atmosphere for meditation . . . or for activities requiring concentration." But green on the ceiling,
. . . think of that—a green ceiling, . . . that can create a reflection on the skin that looks unhealthy, . . . so it can be rather disturbing to people.

Review/study questions or summaries	Notes from class
What are the different locations you can put color indoors?	Color placement - diff. effects Floor, Walls, Ceiling
What effect does yellow generally have indoors? What are the best locations for yellow?	Yellow - indoors = +/happy atmosphere Flr distracting + irritating Wall < light + energy Ceiling " "
What effect does green generally have indoors?	Green - indoors → good concentration/meditation Flr (if nat.) soft/relaxing Walls " "
Wilkens' quotation (txtbk) What are the best locations for green?	"good atmos for meditation/concentration" Ceiling - unhealthy skin tone → disturbing

Listen and Take Notes

Make predictions

▷ p. 8

1. Before the lecture, think about everything you have learned and discussed on the topic of interior design. What do you expect to learn more about in the lecture? Write three predictions below. Compare your predictions with a partner.

1. _____

2. _____

3. _____

Follow the lecture

2. Now follow the lecture and take notes. Remember to listen for the lecture language that signals source citation.

3. How well were you able to recognize the lecture language? Check the statement that best describes you. Explain your answer.

I was able to recognize the lecture language for source citation _____.
a. all the time   **b.** sometimes   **c.** none of the time   **d.** not sure

4. Use your notes to answer these questions.

1. What are physical responses to color? What are learned responses?

_____

_____

_____

_____

2. What is the "value" of a color? What effects do different values produce?

_____

_____

_____

3. What are the effects of warm colors? Of cool colors?

_____

_____

_____

_____

4. What are undertones? How can they be used to achieve color harmony?

_____

_____

_____

_____

5. Were you able to answer the questions in Exercise 4 using the information in your notes? Compare your notes with a few other students. Discuss the differences and help each other fill in any missing information. Complete your notes.

6. Work with a partner and take turns. Review your notes from the lecture. Then explain the main points of the lecture to your partner. Talk for 2-3 minutes only.

Discuss the Issues

Discussion Strategy

Support Your Ideas by Paraphrasing and Quoting Others
Just like professors, you will also need to support your ideas with paraphrases and quotations. Use the same phrases that you learned earlier to cite other people's ideas in a classroom discussion.

Cite sources

1. **Review the expressions for citing sources. Do you understand how to use them? Discuss the phrases with a partner, then discuss any questions you have with your classmates.**

   Paraphrasing (not exact words)
   [Source] states/says/suggests/argues/believes that . . .
   In [title], [source] says/states/suggests/argues . . .
   According to [source], . . .
   To paraphrase [source], . . .

   Quoting (exact words)
   [Source] says, and I quote, "_____."
   [Source] said, quote, "_____."
   In the words of [source], "_____."
   To quote [source], "_____."
   This is what [source] calls "_____."

   _____

   _____

   _____

2. **With a partner, practice the phrases for citing sources. Start by telling your partner an idea or fact from the reading, the practice lecture, the lecture, or any of the transcripts in this chapter. Then use the language for citing sources to support your point.**

   Example:
   *I was surprised to learn that white is not usually a good color for interior walls. In the practice lecture, the professor told us that, **according to Mahnke**, white walls hurt the eyes and affect people badly psychologically.*

3. In groups of four, read the following quotations about art and discuss them. Introduce and cite the idea first as a quotation and then explain it as a paraphrase. Keep the conversation going until every student has had a chance to practice citing sources.

Why do two colors, put one next to the other, sing? Can one really explain this? No. Just as one can never learn how to paint.

Pablo Picasso

Photography is more than a medium for factual communication of ideas. It is a creative art.

Ansel Adams

Art is not what you see, but what you make others see.

Edgar Degas

The moment you think you understand a great work of art, it's dead for you.

Oscar Wilde

To me, art…must be simple in its presentation and direct in its expression, like the language of Nature.

Mohandas Gandhi

4. Discuss these ideas from the lecture with your classmates. Remember to use the phrases for citing sources in your discussion.

1. The lecturer talks about how some color associations are learned. What is your favorite color? What associations do you have with that color—both personal and cultural?

2. Imagine you are part of a design team. In your group decide what would be the best color and type of line for the following interior spaces: a child's playroom, a doctor's office, a workout room or gym, the chapel at a hospital.

3. Which quote from Exercise 3, above, do you most agree with? Why? Do you disagree with any of them? Why or why not?

4. Look back at your notes. What was another idea in the lecture that you found important and interesting? Tell the class why you think it is important or interesting and ask for their opinions.

Unit Wrap-Up

1. **Go online and research Keith Haring or Barry McGee. Find out more about a particular piece, or an event or exhibition he was part of. Share the information and your reactions with the class. Support your research with one or two images.**

2. **Conduct a survey to find out how people in your community feel about graffiti.**

   • Ask at least ten people this question: Does graffiti have a mostly positive or mostly negative effect on the appearance of the community and the community itself? Why do you think so?

   • Compare the results of different age groups (15–24, 25–40, and over 40) and genders.

   Share your results in a small group. Do your results match those of the others in the group? What conclusions can you draw from your overall results? Share your conclusions with the class.

3. **In small groups, choose a room at your institution (classroom, library, etc.) or in your community (hotel lobby, interior of a bank, etc.) to critique.**

   • On your own, think about what the room is used for and then decide how well the use of line, color, and other features suit the room. Make a list of suggestions for how the room might be improved.

   • Discuss your suggestions in your small group. Come to a consensus on how to redo the room. Take photos and/or sketch the room and then make a drawing incorporating your ideas. Share your ideas with the class.

   Notes: _____

   _____

   _____

   _____

   _____

   _____

Teacher's Notes

Organization of the Book

Lecture Ready 3: Strategies for Academic Listening, Note-taking, and Discussion contains five units with two chapters in each unit. Each unit focuses on one field of academic study. Each chapter is built around a lecture from a typical course within the field. In each chapter, students are presented with and practice listening, note-taking, and discussion strategies.

Chapter Guide

Strategy Boxes

Throughout the book, strategies are presented and explained in strategy boxes. These boxes are tabbed within each chapter for easy navigation. After a strategy is introduced, it is recycled in subsequent chapters. At each instance of recycling, a page number tab in the left margin directs students to the original strategy box for quick reference.

Build Background Knowledge

The purpose of this part of the chapter is to introduce the topic and help students think about what they already know so that they can be more active listeners during the lecture.

Think about the topic

In this section, students activate current knowledge of the chapter topic and begin to build understanding and topic vocabulary. Students look at a visual prompt and answer questions about it in order to share information. Encourage broad discussion— there are no right or wrong answers.

Read

The readings employ common academic formats and are based on information from authentic sources. They introduce information that is relevant to the topic of the lecture but not the main ideas of the lecture. The readings also present some of the key vocabulary from the lecture in context. Students should read for general comprehension.

Check your comprehension

This aims to reinforce students' comprehension of the larger ideas in the reading. Again, the goal is to help them build background knowledge about the ideas in the coming lecture.

Expand your vocabulary

Words and phrases from the reading that will be used in the lecture are addressed here. These words and phrases are important for understanding the key ideas in the lecture. In most cases, they come from the **Academic Word List**, so learning them will be valuable for future academic pursuits as well.

Discuss the reading

This continues to build background knowledge and add to what they know about the topic. These questions are designed to get students to react with opinions and personal experiences related to the ideas in the readings. Students do not need to reference the reading; instead, an open-ended discussion should be encouraged.

Review what you know

This is a strategy that good listeners employ automatically: They consciously think about what they know in preparation for taking in new information. Rather than having students begin listening right after they build background knowledge, students are directed to take a moment to collect their background knowledge. They will revisit this section before they watch the lecture.

Prepare to Listen and Take Notes

This part has two purposes: to present the targeted lecture language for that chapter, and to present note-taking strategies.

Lecture Language: Students learn about and practice the strategy of recognizing lecture language—the specific expressions that professors use to guide students through the ideas in the lecture. This language, which can be found in lectures from all disciplines, ranges from expressions that signal the topic of a lecture to non-verbal expressions that signal when a piece of information is important.

Note-taking Strategy: Students learn about and practice a specific note-taking strategy. These strategies range from using a simple outline form to citing sources in your notes.

Prepare to Listen and Take Notes sometimes starts with an activity that introduces the chapter listening strategy in a friendly way. Thinking about the situation helps students discover the need for learning the listening strategy featured in the chapter. Give students time to discuss the situation with a partner before they share with the class.

Listening strategy

Have students read the Listening Strategy box. Then have students work with the set of lecture language expressions. You can have students read the expressions and add others to the list. Or you can first elicit the expressions that students know already. Then look at the list to confirm what they know and add others.

Students practice recognizing the chapter's lecture language in a printed excerpt before listening to the practice lecture. You may prefer to work with the excerpt as a class, using an overhead transparency.

Listen for lecture language

Students listen to a short practice lecture related to the centerpiece lecture. This practice lecture uses simplified content so that students can focus on listening for the target lecture language.

Students listen first for content, in order to understand the ideas. After this activity, have students share their answers with the class to gain confidence.

Students then listen a second time in order to focus on recognizing the chapter lecture language. Since the listening focus is so specific, you might

need to replay the practice lecture in order for student to catch all the instances asked for. First, have students listen and write down only the target lecture language. Then have them listen again and write down the information referenced by the target lecture language.

Note-taking strategy

Have students study the Note-taking Strategy box. In chapter 2, students learn a body of note-taking symbols and abbreviations. In other chapters, students analyze the note-taking strategy by examining an example of student notes that employ the strategy. You might want to show these sample notes on a transparency and point out the specific features of the note-taking strategy.

Students then practice the note-taking strategy by reading an excerpt from a lecture and taking notes on it. Have students compare their notes in pairs.

Listen and Take Notes

In this part, students put their new strategies to work by watching an actual lecture and taking notes on it.

Make predictions

The section begins with a prediction activity. The purpose of this exercise is to remind students of their earlier topic work and help them prepare to take in new information.

Follow the lecture

Students are now ready to "attend" the lecture. In Chapters 1 and 2, a note-taking outline has been provided to guide students toward the key ideas in the lecture. These outlines help them focus their listening and provide a structure for their notes. By Chapter 3 students are taking notes unaided.

Assess your comprehension

After the lecture, students assess three key components: their comprehension of lecture language, their general understanding of some of the key points in the lecture, and their notes.

First, they evaluate their own understanding of the lecture language and tie their comprehension of the lecture to their ability to follow the lecture language.

Students then answer basic comprehension questions about the larger ideas in the lecture using their notes. Encourage students to share their answers and also to explain how they arrived at their answer—to explain what the lecturer actually said.

Next, students assess their notes to see what information they might have missed or misunderstood. Encourage students to discuss the differences in their respective notes and try to understand why they missed or mistook something.

Summarize the lecture

Here, students summarize the lecture to consolidate what they have learned and find out how well they have understood the important ideas in the lecture. The goal is to enhance comprehension of important ideas in the lecture by putting them in their own words. Summarizing the lecture aloud with a partner gives students training in an authentic academic activity—comparing and discussing notes with a classmate. Summarizing is an important strategy that will be useful throughout their academic careers.

Explain to the students that, if they find they have too little to say, this is a good sign that they missed information and should look back at their notes. Point out that they do not need a partner to summarize. This is an excellent strategy to use on their own.

Discuss the Issues

This part is aimed at providing students with appropriate words and phrases for classroom or small-group discussion of the ideas in a lecture. In doing so, these strategies also inform students about the basic expectations for participation and conduct in a discussion setting. Like the listening and note-taking strategies, discussion strategies become progressively more sophisticated, going from "entering a discussion" to "supporting your own ideas by paraphrasing and quoting others."

Discussion strategy

Have students read the Discussion Strategy box. Then have students work with the set of discussion expressions. You can have students read the expressions and add others to the list. Or you can first elicit the expressions that students know already. Then look at the list to confirm what they know and add others.

Discussion practice

In this role-play activity, students are given the chance to practice the discussion language in a more guided way. The content in this section is easily accessible so that the focus can be on practicing the discussion language. Be sure to monitor the groups as they do their role-plays and hold students accountable for their use of the discussion language.

Discuss the ideas in the lecture

Students now bring all their knowledge of the content and the discussion strategy together in a real classroom or small-group discussion of ideas in the lecture. Encourage them to have their lecture notes with them, as they should refer to actual lecture content when appropriate. Encourage students to use the discussion language they have just learned. You may want to appoint a group member to keep track of this.

Unit Wrap-Up

At the end of each unit (so, at the end of every second chapter), there is a Unit Wrap-Up that aims to get students to synthesize the topics in the two chapters and think more conceptually and critically about the broader theme. You can assign these activities or not—they are not strictly part of the units or chapters.

Students get a taste of academic project work such as planning and carrying out a survey, drawing conclusions from survey data, presenting their findings and conclusions before an audience, preparing an argument for or against a topic in a debate.

About the Authors

Laurie Frazier

Laurie Frazier is Instructional Consultant at the Center for Teaching and Learning Services at the University of Minnesota. She teaches courses and consults with international graduate students and scholars on classroom communication skills and strategies for teaching in a US academic environment. Previously, she taught ESL at several California institutions: City College of San Francisco, Mission College in Santa Clara, and the American Language Institute at San Francisco State University. She has a Master's Degree in TESOL from San Francisco State University. Laurie is co-author of *Lecture Ready 3*.

Shalle Leeming

Shalle Leeming has prepared students for academic study in English and trained teachers on four continents. She has taught university-level EFL and ESL at several institutions, including Kwansei Gakuin University in Nishinomiya, Japan, Koç University in Istanbul, Turkey, and two San Francisco Bay Area universities: Stanford University and the American Language Institute at San Francisco State University. She is currently an instructor and faculty developer at the Academy of Art University in San Francisco. She holds a Master's Degree in TESOL from San Francisco State University. Shalle is co-author of *Lecture Ready 3*.

Peg Sarosy

Peg Sarosy is an Academic Coordinator at the American Language Institute at San Francisco State University. She previously taught at San Francisco State University in the ESL department and the Design and Industry department. She taught academic preparation at the University of California - Berkeley intensive English program and was a USIS Teacher Trainer in the Czech Republic. She has a Master's Degree in TESOL from San Francisco State University. Peg is co-author of *Lecture Ready 1* and *Lecture Ready 2,* and a series editor for *Lecture Ready 3*.

Kathy Sherak

Kathy Sherak is Director of the American Language Institute at San Francisco State University. She previously taught in San Francisco State University's ESL program and was a Fulbright Teacher Trainer in Italy. She is the author of the Teacher's Manual for *Grammar Sense Book 3* from Oxford University Press. She has a Master's Degree in TESOL from San Francisco State University. Kathy is co-author of *Lecture Ready 1* and *Lecture Ready 2,* and a series editor for *Lecture Ready 3*.

Notes

Notes

Notes

Notes

Notes

Notes